Naturalistic Gardening

Naturalistic Gardening

Reflecting

the Planting Patterns

of Nature

Ann Lovejoy
Photographs by Allan Mandell

SASQUATCH BOOKS
SEATTLE

For Elizabeth England, mentor and guide whose vision,
understanding, and standards elevated the practice of horticulture for a generation
of West Coast gardeners, and for all the generous, talented, skillful gardeners who
shared their explorations of the concepts behind this book.
—A. L.

I would like to dedicate this book to the memory of Elizabeth England,
a guiding figure in the Victoria, B.C., community. I had the privilege of photographing
her garden in its final moments of peak form, an eloquent statement of her life's
work. Elizabeth helped bring my work to a higher level, so that the heart
and spirit of the gardener play a much greater role in my vision.
—A. M.

Contents

Introduction

Introduction

Naturalistic gardening is not natural. Indeed, as any gardener is acutely aware, gardening is by definition interference with nature. Until very recently, there has been precious little of the natural to be found in any

"proper" garden. Gardens that displayed more than their share of nature were considered to be neglected, distressed, or simply abandoned. Over the past century, the idea of wild gardening arose almost simultaneously in

England, Europe, and North America. Based at least in part upon natural habitats and native plants, this radical school offered us several vital concepts.

First, the idea of cooperative gardening involves working *with* rather than *against* plants by acknowledging their natural inclinations. Cooperative gardening consists further of placing our plants where nature would best have them (in terms of size, habit, and life span). Cooperative gardening is sometimes called the "right plant, right place" school, in that intelligent plant placement solves persistent garden problems, such as those caused by boggy or dry sites.

Naturalistic garden plantings are built upon the architectural attributes of the selected plants, and partnerships are designed to call out essential qualities of form and texture rather than to focus chiefly on colorist effects. The result can be amazingly powerful and remain beautiful for months on end.

Editing is another important element in wild gardening. For purists, the difference between natural habitat and a wild garden may be little more than grooming the woods: removing fallen limbs and browned fern fronds, and judiciously pruning native shrubs to repair weather damage. For others, wild gardening means using native and non-native plants to enhance a natural setting. Still another definition involves evoking the feeling of natural plantings in places where real nature has been eradicated (urban and suburban sites). For the average gardener, the idea of wild gardening may come down to helping nature out a little when selectivity issues crop up (such as whether a crop of foxglove seedlings should be left or removed).

Naturalistic gardening is a bit different, expanding upon all of these basic concepts in several directions. It is largely a North American phenomenon, and one that has its origins in the Western states. This is not an accident. For many generations now, the restless and the rule breakers have headed west, along with the curious and the novelty seekers. Over time a Western sensibility and attitude have developed in which flexibility, creativity, and ingenuity are prized and the new and nontraditional are preferred.

It is not, therefore, surprising that a great many fresh ideas should germinate in such a creative environment. Western garden design reflects that richness, and contemporary gardens from Denver to Seattle and British Columbia to San Francisco are setting new standards of style and plantsmanship. These naturalistic gardens are based in large part upon the relationships and layering found in natural plant communities. Interlayered plantings of whatever kind are intended to echo the physical partnerships and social structures (in terms of commonly related plant communities) that we see repeated over and over in an enormous variety of natural settings and habitats.

For instance, in the Pacific Northwest, alders, vine maples, wild cherries, and madronas are common canopy partners, often accompanied by understory colonies of redtwig dogwood, Indian plum, and hazels. Beneath that layer are found carpets of salal punctuated by mahonias and huckleberries. The exact mix of such typical communities reflects factors such as soil type, light, moisture, and so forth, but variations on these partnerships are extremely common. In naturalistic gardens, canopy trees are similarly interwoven with understory shrubs, perennials, and ground covers. Naturalistic gardeners seek to combine their plants in ways that echo those natural planting patterns and similarly accentuate their essential qualities and characteristics. The plants are also placed in situations that will please them, and are given like-minded company, which helps to assure healthy plants and reduces the amount of work (or interference) required from the gardener.

The goal of reducing the gardener's labor is not driven by sheer laziness (though laziness can spark some very efficient ideas), but by pragmatism. The traditional gardens of England and Europe were made by and for people who could assume that a large and inexpensive supply of skilled labor would always be on tap. Here and now, that is just

Traditional design styles often ignore the natural regional vernacular even when garden areas adjoin significant habitat. Most emphasize obvious control measures such as clipping or shearing rather than celebrating the authentic character of garden plants that create a visual link with the adjacent landscape.

not true. Most of us do much or all of our own work in the garden, and when we do find help, the helpers are not likely to be well trained (which in no way implies that they won't be expensive). Therefore, we need gardens that we can take care of with relative ease, and that won't make us feel guilty when we can't make the time. We need to create gardens that don't really need us very much. Such independence is of course relative—all gardens need periodic care and editing, or they would not be gardens. However, thoughtful planning and realistic assessment of our plants' propensities can save us an amazing amount of unnecessary work. What *is* necessary can then be done on our schedules, without pressure or the risk of ruining the look of the garden for a full season through untimely neglect.

Toward this worthy goal, many traditional ideas and techniques are modified to make gardening less mysterious and more satisfying. In design terms, naturalistic gardens are simple and uncluttered, their lines based on gentle curves and sweeps rather than straight lines and geometrical axes. Their proportions of path and bed are generous and related to the scale of the largest plant elements, without emulating the typical sterile, parklike plantings seen in many public and estate gardens, which lack any distinct character or personality. Frames and backdrops are created not with objects but with plants, chiefly evergreens, which are unclipped and soft in outline. The backdrop plantings are built up in ruffled, irregular tiers rather than formal or neatly stacked stair steps. Any unavoidable hard edges, whether from walls or fences, are disguised when possible with living drapery, preferably evergreen.

In planting style, naturalistic gardens may be simple or very complex indeed, but the interior patterns are always plant dominated. The concept of planting within beds and borders is retained from the English and European styles, but within them, the shape, size, texture, and mass of each plant is at least as important to the overall composition as the colors involved. English and European beds are often framed by lawns, but in naturalistic gardens lawn is disappearing fast. Turf, which requires constant upkeep and looks utterly artificial, is rejected in favor of graveled sweeps and large mixed plantings divided by paths (also graveled or barked) and seating areas.

Perhaps most important of all, nearly all naturalistic gardens are personal, and many are very small. These are not sweeping estates or great parcels of habitat, nor are they large parks maintained by a staff. Some have had the benefit of professional guidance and assistance, but the essential flavor in each is that of the pleasurable relationship between the gardener and the plants, the gardener and the created environment.

In Europe and England, the idea of "natural" gardening has led to the development of a variety of styles, none of them precisely the same as North American naturalistic, and all of them more deeply wedded to the formal. The eye so trained requires the comfort of familiarity, and even in the so-called natural English gardens, you will still see those "natural" borders surrounded by flat lawns like billiard tables and precisely clipped hedges or walls, which are felt necessary to balance the less structured plantings. Looked at dispassionately, most of these gardens are really quite stiff and contrived, reflecting more about their planners than the character and spirit of the plants themselves. There is nothing wrong with all that control, except when the unconscious assumption that this pattern is "right" causes its advocates to see less formally framed styles and settings as "wrong."

According to the sculptor and painter George Little, a garden artist who often works with plant shapes, the importance of naturalistic gardening lies in the principle of layering. "When we make gardens, we are working with space, living space, in two senses," he notes. "First, the garden is alive, made up of living things. Second, it's a living space, like a living room. Layering our plants creates an atmosphere of living space. Giving it that living quality is what engages our imagination; it's like working with a friend. That imaginative bond makes gardening more of an exchange between you and your plants."

What's more, the negative space in a composition is as important as the plants, George reminds us, and a vital visual element in plant placement. The space we leave between the plants is what allows us to see their shapes as well as the patterns they make together. When plants are set as closely together as they often are in colorist borders, their colors take precedence over form. In naturalistic borders the alternating shapes of the plants are woven together in ways that create an intriguing interior topography. Planting to emphasize shape also triggers a fascinating physical interplay as plants chase each other in and out of front positions over the seasons, often alternating roles, so that a given plant is now a star, now subsidiary.

George Little also stresses the importance of the visionary imagination when placing plants. "A lot of people have a hard time trusting themselves, but to make art, garden art or any kind, you have to trust your instincts. Go with your gut feeling, balancing that with what you know about a plant."

His partner, David Lewis, agrees vigorously, adding, "And if you don't know enough about the plant, find out more." He also believes that layering is a vital piece of naturalistic garden making. He explains, "Layering encourages the movement of the eye through and beyond the garden. Those stacks of limbs and branches lead the eye up to the sky and back down to the earth. Because it reminds us of nature, the layered look is comforting to the eye. In fact, it works indoors and out; whether we are organizing household ornaments or art objects or plants or garden art, it's all based on intuitive patterns and relationships that can be best understood in terms of layers."

In native habitat, trees, shrubs, perennials, and ground covers are woven into a dense, textured tapestry whose ruffled layers lead the eye up to the trees and back to the ground.

Gardening in Layers

Gardening in Layers

chapter 1

Though the idea of gardening with layered plantings may sound new, it is at heart an extension or amplification of what many gardeners already do by instinct. Simply stated, layering involves the grouping of garden plants not only by size, but also by associations that are similar to those found in natural plant communities. The skyline plant layer consists generally of trees, whose silhouettes can be seen against the sky from a distance. Next come tall understory plants, usually a mixture of shrubs and large perennials. Beneath these are mid-level plants, a role often filled by perennials. Last come the carpeters, plants that cover the ground.

For ornamental garden models, the layering prototype is a mature woodland. Here, the largest trees soar above intermediate shrubs. Beneath these are ranged clumps and flowing masses of perennials. At their base run spreading carpets of ground-covering plants. These carpets are often punctuated by colonies of seasonal bulbs, and the overall woodland community may be laced

This naturalistic garden enriches a foundation of native trees, shrubs, and ground covers with bog-loving perennials like these candelabra primulas (*Primula beesiana* and hybrids). Bigleaf maple (*Acer macrophyllum*) and red elder (*Sambucus racemosa*) punctuate the carpet of mosses, sword ferns (*Polystichum munitum*), and lacy lady ferns (*Athyrium filix-femina*). Weesjes garden, North Saanich, British Columbia.

Naturalistic layering creates an interplay and flow of form within the borders that remind the eye of the relationships seen in natural plant communities. Here ornamental sages rise like blue water above low, grey-blue ruffles of sea kale *(Crambe maritima)*, while a sheaf of chartreuse euphorbia echoes in miniature the soft spikes of a lemony tree lupine farther down the border. The wall is softened with a lush blanket of variegated canary ivy *(Hedera algeriensis)*, a tender creeper that appreciates the reflected warmth it gets here, framed between the house and the asphalt driveway. Garden of Valerie Murray, Victoria, British Columbia.

together by clambering vines. The exact makeup of these plant communities differs from place to place, yet the overall relationships remain fairly constant.

In North American woodlands, from the open forests of New England and the northern tier states to the lush Northwestern rain forest or the dense, moss-hung woods of the Deep South, the canopy is a rich mixture of deciduous and evergreen trees. Where winters are harsh, the evergreens will chiefly be conifers, while more temperate regions boast broad-leaved evergreen trees as well. Woodland shrubs present a similar blending of evergreen and deciduous, and the percentages of each are roughly equivalent in all settings, although the variety of broad-leaved evergreens is greatest where winters are mild. Perennial herbs occur in relative profusion everywhere, as do bulbs and vines.

Where formal or obviously artificial gardens may charm or stimulate, they very rarely comfort us or make us feel welcome. Natural woodlands, however, have become a visual cliché in wall posters because to the average viewer, they denote inner peace as successfully as a calm sea suggests serenity. If such a greeting-card sensibility seems overly romantic or even sentimental, it nonetheless points toward a genuine and verifiable human response to the natural. Over the past several decades, numerous stress-response tests have demonstrated that when humans are shown pictures of natural settings, we relax measurably. In fact, people who can look at plants out of their office windows have lower heart rates, better immune system function, and experience less stress than those who view man-made objects.

This research prompts the suggestion that gardens intended to be meditative or peaceful havens be made as "green" as possible, combining the plants in those comforting layers we observe in the natural plant communities. It seems likely that gardens enclosed with green layers, rather than clipped hedges or hard-edged walls, would have the same soothing effect on human psyches. We could then fill our beds and borders in whatever manner we chose, gaining both the psychological and physical benefits of a green enclosure while providing a visually effective backing for our more colorful seasonal compositions.

Emulating Natural Layers

When we emulate those natural layers of canopy, tall and compact understory, and ground covers in our gardens, we don't have to try to copy them exactly, or attempt to replicate habitat. We may choose to do so, of course, but if we prefer instead to make gardens that reflect any of a variety of long-established styles or modes, we can still capture the feeling of naturalness that characterizes those native plantings by adapting the lush layering and interplay of plants. Not only will we benefit in health and well-being, but by replacing clipped hedges with unshaped ones, we also save ourselves a significant amount of needless labor.

Naturalistic layering is *not* about the strict ranking of plants by height, placing larger ones at the back and stepping them down in orderly fashion until the border edges (which in traditional styles are probably trimmed with tightly clipped boxwood). It is most definitely not about ranking woody plants (often chosen for values other than natural size) in this manner, then controlling any tendency for them to outgrow their position through annual pruning or more frequent shearing. This illogical but widespread concept remains powerfully influential in European, English, and North American formal garden design, where the hand of man is very much apparent.

Over the centuries, traditional English and European garden design has stressed this kind of controlling role, reflecting a shared religious doctrine that emphasized man's supremacy over nature. Until very recently, most church teachings implicitly suggested that the natural world was created in order to serve humanity. Since the church loomed very large in both English and European cultures, its attitudes strongly affected the way most people viewed nature, and by extension, their gardens and the entire plant kingdom.

Among those who favor formalism, the classic stair-step approach to plant placement is still popular. Over the past few decades, however, revolutionary garden designers have suggested discovering and responding to the natural conditions presented by a garden site, rather than imposing a design that has nothing to do with the physical realities of the setting.

For instance, across Lake Washington from Seattle, the Northwest Perennial Alliance has created an internationally renowned set of mixed borders that contain over ten thousand kinds of plants in naturalistic combinations. English visitors in particular have been smitten with what they consider a radical design. The main borders encompass some 17,000 square feet, all of which is densely interplanted in architectural combinations and vignettes. The heart of the border is accessible by a narrow path that allows visitors to be enveloped by the sheer vigor of the magnificent plantings. When he saw them, Ray Lancaster (noted English author, lecturer, and plantsman extraordinaire) commented that in England, nobody would even think of making a border that follows the natural contours of a sloping hillside as this one does. He was also moved by the uncommon beauty of plants seen silhouetted against the sky from a pathway some 10 feet below the border's top level, a refreshing viewpoint that traditional flat borders cannot offer.

In the Pacific Northwest, and increasingly elsewhere in North America, gardeners are seeking out plants that will adapt readily to the cultural conditions of their gardens, rather than trying to create an artificially homogeneous situation. (Here again, standard practice required us to alter our native soils as best we might, in order to create that mythical well-drained yet moisture retentive soil that is supposed to delight the most difficult border beauties.) More and more, gardeners are trying to work with their plants rather than force arbitrary roles upon them. Until recently, few people would think twice about using what are potentially huge trees as foundation plantings or hedges. When the tree-character of those plants asserted itself, the typical response was simply to hack off any piece that didn't fit the chosen shape or pattern. Almost nobody questioned the need or good sense of this very common routine, including garden writers and designers, despite the reams of garden writing that explained in laborious depth how to compensate the wounded plants for that indignity. Nearly universal cultural assumptions blinded us to the silliness of our intellectual slavery to such traditional

The informality of planting that characterizes naturalistic gardens does not mean that they will appear untidy. Rather, their implied sense of a natural order is simply less restrictive than that in formally designed spaces. A flow of clematis softens the stern line of the enclosing fence, which is stepped to follow the fall of the land as well as to reduce the harshness of line. In the borders, broad blue hostas are threaded with lacy golden feverfew, making contrasts of form and texture as well as color. Along the winding path, bushy spills of golden oregano spread in smooth, stonelike mounds to enhance the fluid clematis vine behind them. Garden of Elizabeth England, Victoria, British Columbia.

Thoughtful placement enables naturalistic designers to combine plants of all kinds in lastingly cooperative communities. When selected with care, trees and shrubs do not outgrow their position or company even in maturity. Here the native woods merge into the garden at its edges, while the sunny interior holds border plants from all over the temperate world. Hostas, rodgersias, and alchemillas spill over the gravel pathway, while dwarf fruit trees and choice Japanese maples create sculptural shapes within the borders. Garden of Carmen Varcoe, Victoria, British Columbia.

but exceedingly illogical plant choices—most particularly silly when we live thousands of miles away from the lands where those choices might have been sensible ones. (Although quite often they were no more sensible even then.)

Sensible, Sensitive Planting

Today, enlightened practice directs us to seek out plants that will not outgrow their positions. Rather than trying to keep a Douglas fir hedge 10 feet tall, we would select instead an evergreen hedge shrub that matures at 10 feet. To avoid endless trimming and clipping, we would choose

a plant with a handsome natural shape. In fact, because the average hedge run changes character over its length, often dramatically, we would ideally select an assortment of compatible plants, evergreen and deciduous, and weave them into tapestry hedges, rather than try to make one kind of plant adapt to the whole range of conditions.

By selecting plants intelligently and placing them with thoughtful attention to real needs and conditions, we are not pitting ourselves against those plants but working cooperatively with them. In the same way, when we array our plants in layers, we seek to recreate the soft-edged look of natural plant communities in which each plant chose its own spot. Near my house is an open meadow bordered by a woodland. I pass this scene daily, sometimes many times a day, and have seen it in every season, every light, and every weather. Those mixed woods inspired my year-round mixed borders, and continue to inspire the gardens I am making today.

In these woods and the accompanying meadow, each plant seems brilliantly placed for maximum beauty. Clumps of redtwig dogwoods, *Cornus stolonifera*, create a running thicket that suddenly gives way to flurries of fine textured *Spiraea douglasii* and Indian plum *(Oemleria cerasiformis)*. Above them rise matching thickets of slim alders, punctuated at perfect intervals by vine maples, honey locust, or cascara. The patterns shift back and forth between the densely twiggy and more open architecture, each in precisely the proper proportion to best accentuate their own qualities as well as their neighbor's. Indeed, plants in nature quite often are brilliantly placed, for given the chance, they will put themselves exactly where they can grow best. They will also, of course, put themselves in quite a few less than optimal spots. It is a mistake

In my own backyard, a patch of native woods is incorporated into the garden. The transitional plantings (shown a few months after planting) will fill in quickly, and within a year the edge of the woodland will be disguised. The moss-encrusted nurse log hosts glossy native salal *(Gaultheria shallon)*, sword ferns *(Polystichum munitum)*, and both evergreen and deciduous huckleberries *(Vaccinium ovatum* and *V. parvifolium*, respectively), as well as holly-like, low-growing leatherleaf *(Mahonia repens)* and the upright Oregon grape *(M. aquifolium)*. Native ground covers include wood sorrel *(Oxalis oregana)*, fringecup *(Tellima grandiflora)*, and piggyback plant *(Tolmiea menziesii)*, a common houseplant in cooler climes. Lovejoy/Rogers garden, Bainbridge Island, Washington.

to idealize nature, for in her extraordinary abundance, she strews her offspring with such abandon that the result is rather hit-or-miss. If we want to keep our garden plants in

harmonious balance, we must edit as ruthlessly as do natural forces—wind, disease, fire, rot—in the wild.

Ideally, naturalistic layering patterns will guide us to place not only the woody, structural plants but every plant where its natural shape, height, and mass are precisely what our design requires. For instance, when we want a slim, upright shape, we will choose a plant that will retain that shape throughout its life, rather than selecting something that must repeatedly be pruned into the desired shape. We seek also to place each plant so that its innate architectural qualities will be expressed. Color, texture, flower, and foliage color are all taken into consideration as well, but the emphasized quality will always be that of the plant's overall essence, its most pronounced characteristic.

In order to use plants intelligently and to their best advantage, the designer is required to know a good deal about a great many plants. What's more, we need to know how they are likely to respond in a number of different sites and settings. This may seem daunting, but gardeners who grow and learn about a wide range of plants will have an edge over those who stick with a mere handful. So to

The most effective and lastingly lovely naturalistic gardens are designed by those who take both pleasure and risks in their placement. Native trees make living columns atop a dramatic bank, which is richly layered in a sumptuous mixture of evergreens and deciduous shrubs that retain their basic shapes and textures in every season. This structural planting frames the entryway to a hillside garden, effectively capitalizing on the steep slope created by leveling the driveway. Israelit garden, designed by Michael Schultz, Portland, Oregon.

expand our effective palette, we have to experiment with as many plants as possible. It's a tough job, but . . . In any of the lively arts, the best work comes from those who know their medium so thoroughly that they can call out the fullest potential in their chosen materials. The result is always more lastingly beautiful than work that is done brilliantly but without respect for the natural proclivities of the medium.

The Pleasure Principle

If artful gardening sounds like a lot of work, take heart. Every stage, from plan to finished product, is really quite a lot of fun. If to further our knowledge we must grow a wide variety of plants, then every garden needs its nursery bed and test plot, where new and unfamiliar plants can be trialed before their incorporation into the beds and borders. This of course means finding a spot for the R & D department, but with a little ingenuity even tiny gardens can encompass a test plot.

When I gardened in the city and my children were very small, their sandbox doubled in winter as a cutting bed/cold frame and nest for new plants. When I couldn't squeeze another plant into the ground, I found an old, tiered plant stand that took up very little ground space but held over thirty pots. Buying every new and wonderful plant that calls your name is a tall order, I know, yet we simply have to shoulder this burden if we want to stretch past our comfort zone and grow along with our gardens.

What we want for and from our gardens is in the process of changing more rapidly and dramatically than it has for many years. We are looking for ways to garden that do not adversely affect the piece of land in our care. We are also exploring ways to combine plants in groupings that make cultural sense, and take full advantage of their specific beauties. What's more, we increasingly want our gardens to present enticing vignettes in every season. Where winters are mild, we want the garden to remain alive and full of change even during the off-months.

We will make mistakes along the way, but nothing is quite so instructive. When we commit horticultural errors, the result can teach us a great deal about both what we like and what we don't like. If we like something, we tend not to investigate further. When we are less satisfied, we put more effort into discovering what went wrong and what is required to make it right.

Naturally, we will be doing a fair amount of editing and rearranging as our plants respond to their homesite and their neighbors. A good gardener once told me that all perennials should come with wheels. Mixed border builders would expand this to say that all plants should come with hand trucks (and it would be nice if they could bring their own holes, too). Our initial editing will be inspired by errors, but plant maturity and refinements of our own taste can necessitate change as well. No matter how or in what style we choose to garden, the odds of getting it "right" the first time we plant are approximately nil. Only in extremely formal bedding-out, where your best friend is your ruler, is there a fighting chance of placing everything to your satisfaction the first time around, and that only works because it's an artificial pattern, based on geometry or symmetry or numbers, not taking into account the vagaries of site, setting, and the realities of the plants you have to work with.

Artful garden planning must also take into account our own changes—not simply maturing taste and more informed plant choices, but our own changing bodies. Phoebe Noble, an astronomer and extraordinary gardener now in her eighties, explained recently that she has been watching the composition and style of her large (and rather famous) garden alter slowly with the years. "Originally, the garden had quite a few formal areas, with clipped hedges, tightly mown lawns, and long borders that needed hand weeding," she recalls. That has been changing recently, and though she still has some hedges clipped each year, she finds herself enjoying the more natural look that is developing where the enclosing trees and shrubs are left unclipped. In some of the woodsier sections, where many native plants now grow, the garden looks like a well-edited extension of the native woods, remnants of which surround this large suburban garden.

Some years ago Mrs. Noble decided that she could no longer keep up the heavy maintenance required by formal beds. She redesigned several large sections of the garden, including an old orchard that holds hundreds of species and hybrid geraniums, to be less demanding and simpler in upkeep. Paths were widened to permit free passage of the

Naturalistic plant placement can be both colorful and playful, reflecting the designer's delight in combining well-grown plants into like-minded communities. The young hedge has not yet achieved the intended total enclosure, but already it provides visual screening for neighboring houses as well as a buffer for ocean winds. In its protective embrace, the ruddy, strap-leaved New Zealand flax *(Phormium tenax)* will develop its distinctive natural form without windburn or shredding. Whitehead garden, Sidney, British Columbia.

large, sit-down mower, which enables her to keep the 5-acre garden tidy without regular assistance. To eliminate hand edging, the planting beds were rimmed with species and hybrid geraniums (of which she has several hundred), plants that accept mowing with aplomb. In several places native shrubs and perennials that were once routinely removed have been encouraged to cover ground where weeds would otherwise flourish. Although she remains very active in the garden, she is frank about what she can and can't do these days. "I come from long-lived, healthy people, but I had to accept that, realistically, I may only have ten or fifteen years left when I can put in eight or ten hours a day in the garden. That's why I began making real changes, among them letting native plants do more for me."

Naturalistic planting is not about numbing perfectionism but about joyful discovery. There is plenty of room for error, and indeed, accidental combinations and effects are often as good or better than anything we can dream up. They can even rival the effects of nature, which after all contain a good element of accident. A very great designer, Marco Stufano, whose gardens at Wave Hill in the Bronx, New York, are world famous, has often said that gardens that don't take risks aren't worth making. Unless we are willing to try new ideas, new techniques, new plants, and new designs, we can never travel beyond the known.

So we make a few mistakes along the way. So what? Any experimental scientist—or artist—will agree that we learn far more from our mistakes than from easy achievement. When we examine our less-than-perfect efforts, seeking to understand what does and doesn't work, we begin to decipher the roots of our own taste as well as the solid principles of design and composition that underlie both natural and contrived plantings. It is hard to imagine a more pleasurable enterprise, or one that can do more to forward horticultural excellence.

In the old orchard, wide paths and well-planted beds allow much of the maintenance to be carried out with a sit-down mower. The old trees are set off by their understory of hardy geraniums and ornamental onions (*Allium* species), supplemented by interlayered foliage plants such as ferns, hostas, and grasses. The soft, naturalistic tree line is repeated in the beds, where plants are not stair-stepped, but placed informally to create telling contrasts of form, texture, and size. Garden of Phoebe Noble, Sidney, British Columbia.

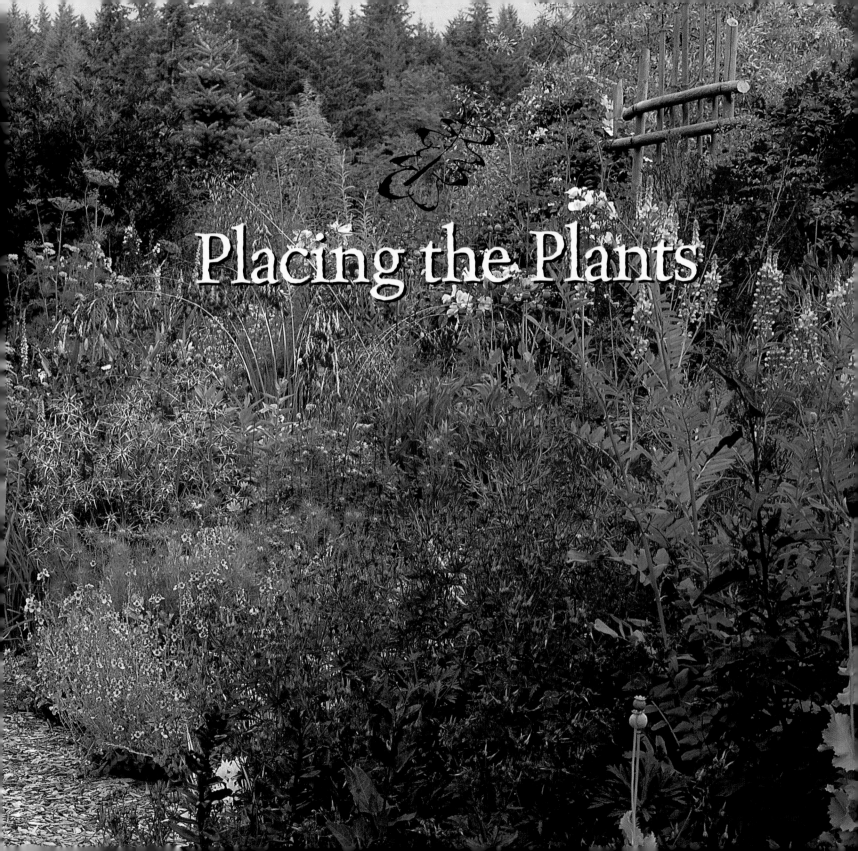

Placing the Plants

Placing the Plants

chapter 2

The way in which naturalistic layering works is quite obvious to both eye and intellect when we look at a natural landscape where trees and shrubs effortlessly combine themselves. In the garden it can be a bit harder to

see. Simply put, layering involves mingling plants of all kinds, not just by size but in appropriate and companionable communities, placing them so that the natural shapes

Native trees and plants form a shell of greenery about a delicious mélange of ornamental shrubs, perennials, and grasses. Plants chosen for their distinctive form and texture are placed to emphasize those inherent qualities. The potent rock shapes do not overwhelm the plantings, which are equally powerful despite their relative softness. Israelit garden, designed by Michael Schultz, Portland, Oregon.

and forms of each plant are emphasized. Trees and shrubs, perennials and annuals, grasses and bulbs, vines and ground covers are woven into mutually supportive groupings, which again are intended to reveal rather than conceal the essential qualities of each component.

In nearly all design styles, traditional and otherwise, enclosure—framing and defining the garden space with walls, hedges, or fences—is a critical concept. This is true of most naturalistic gardens as well, with certain exceptions. Enclosure functions first of all to exclude unwanted sights and sounds from the garden space. It provides visual privacy and gives the garden physical definition, just as walls define house space. In naturalistic layered gardens, enclosure creates a sense of being in a natural environment, protected from the noisy, busy man-made world of machinery and cars. Within living green walls woven from woody plants of various kinds, another more ancient and harmonious world can unfold.

In naturalistic layered gardens, the primary design goal is often to create enclosure for the garden as a whole. Gardens that border large, natural habitat areas very often combine the snug effect of local enclosure (from hedging, for example) near the house with a looser look for outlying areas, particularly those with expansive, territorial views. Such larger-scaled garden areas are partially framed (to preserve those views), using mixed layers of woody plants, often native trees and shrubs. This pattern is also common in seaside gardens and those that overlook rivers or other large bodies of water.

In order to provide effective enclosure without evident artifice, woody plants are arranged in unsheared tapestry hedges around the perimeters of the garden. Tapestry hedges are built up with combinations of evergreen and deciduous trees and shrubs, which can be combined to produce a succession of seasonal flowers and fruits as well as visual screening all year round. Solid evergreen walls rarely look natural, but well-constructed tapestry hedges can create adequate enclosure without requiring shearing or frequent pruning. Between half and two-thirds of the tapestry hedge plants will be either evergreen or so densely twiggy that they provide effective screening and privacy even in winter. Where ground space is limited, most of these enclosing plants will be naturally upright, narrowly columnar, or fastigiate in habit. Because many of us work with modest budgets,

large plants may not be affordable. In such cases, visual privacy may be immediately provided through fencing or staggered rows of tall ornamental grasses (those big miscanthus are terrific for this), with our young hedge plantings arrayed where they will mature into effective screening over time.

Creating Inner Topography

Once enclosure is achieved, the beds and borders are shaped around gently wandering paths. Within these planting areas, compact border shrubs and dwarf conifers are arranged in island clusters that may merge into the tapestry hedges in some places and form freestanding groups in others. These clustered evergreen plantings provide structural presence throughout the year, keeping the borders alive and full even when leaves have fallen and flowers are few. When these groupings are composed chiefly for off-season beauty, they will combine a variety of forms, textures, and colorations as well as contrasting growth habits. These evergreen island clusters become both backdrop and visual support for

---

When territorial and expansive water views are offered to the eye, garden plantings must be boldly architectural in order to successfully compete. Here, citrus-colored *Carex elata* 'Bowles' Golden' gleams beside chartreuse lady's mantle (*Alchemilla mollis*), while down the border, spills of gilded creeping Jenny (*Lysimachia nummularia* 'Aurea') provide a solid underplanting for the shimmering, netted gold of Bowles' golden grass, *Milium effusum* 'Aureum'. Whitehead garden, Sidney, British Columbia.

Enclosure is vital to any garden, setting it apart from the mundane world. Here, loose layers of trees and shrubs blur the straight lines of an enclosing fence. Within the beds, ruffled plantings are similarly layered to mimic the informal tiers of the tapestry hedge. Madrona garden, designed by Michael Schultz & Geoff Beasley, Sherwood, Oregon.

early and late bloomers, besides providing the quiet-season effects dependent on berry, bark, and twig. So, too, do the loose, unclipped hedges, that may not look hedgelike at all to those accustomed to tight shearing. (Naturalistic tapestry hedges are often more reminiscent of the mixed hedgerows found in old English country properties.) Even where snow lies deep all winter, well-orchestrated combinations of such structural plantings will offer understated beauties of form and shadow, and each thaw will reveal a vital, green garden rather than a slumbering grey one.

Balancing Seasonal Flow

In naturalistically layered mixed beds and borders, an effort is generally made to extend the growing season as much as possible, echoing the flow of life and color seen in natural habitats. Most traditional gardens peak in spring or summer, but in mixed border plantings, colorful plants appear, perform, and bow themselves out in steady succession from late winter well into fall. Early bulbs are grouped with later-rising perennials whose leafy stems will disguise the fading bulb foliage. Late bloomers are partnered with plants that experience early dormancy, clearing the way for their neighbor's display. Tidy shrubs buttress tall perennials that would otherwise require staking. Plants that lose their looks after blooming (such as lupines and oriental poppies) are tucked behind protective companions who can emphasize their beauties and minimize their shortcomings. Plants that require frequent grooming (such as daylilies and tea roses) are placed near access paths, so they can be tended without wading through the burgeoning borders.

Plants that retreat or die with elegance and grace can be allowed to remain in place, though only lightly groomed, over a very long season, particularly when their seedheads are as handsome (or nearly so) as their flowers. Brown is a much-neglected color in border work, yet

In order to keep up a steady flow of color and interest, naturalistic gardens incorporate a good percentage of plants that offer attractions in several seasons. Here, muted, old gold fronds of false Solomon's seal are decked with hot red "flowers" as tumbling maple leaves spangle the ground with colorful confetti. Garden of Robin Hopper & Judi Dyelle, Metchosin, British Columbia.

some extremely powerful combinations can be worked by incorporating the full range of biscuit, buff, toast, and sand displayed by ripening and fading seedheads and leaves. Indeed, fall coloring is a further consideration, and not only with woody plants. A surprising number of perennials, from peonies to herb Robert *(Geranium robertianum)*, produce reliably fine autumn foliage color that lasts for weeks.

Making the Most of Plants

In naturalistic gardens, the plants are arranged so that the shape and texture of each makes as important a contribution to the overall composition of the border as the flowers and foliage. The idea is to recognize and take advantage of each plant's architectural qualities; contrast of shape as well as color makes for more visually stimulating combinations that are not dependent on flowers.

Contriving attractive contrasts of the former kind requires us to review our plant list in terms of shape. There are four basic pairs: Fans and fountains are both broader at the top than at the base. Pyramids and spires are broad-based and tapering at the top. Rounded mounds may be stone-smooth and almost hard edged or airily constructed and frothy in texture, while sprawlers spill or tumble with liquid grace. In a class of their own are the eccentrics, potently shaped plants that are not symmetrical. To create powerful contrasts of form, begin playing around with partnerships that combine two, three, or more of these basic shapes.

Many fine gardeners have earned their reputations through inventive combinations of form. In England, Beth Chatto often gives her vignettes a pyramidal or triangular centerpiece, flanking firmly upright plants with softer, mounded ones. Rhythmic repeats of this simple pattern create an intriguing flow of topography throughout the long, running borders in her gardens. In the J. C. Ralston Arboretum at North Carolina State University, Edith Eddleman creates extravagantly splendid borders that emphasize striking contrasts of form as well as marvelous colorist effects. Many plants are oversized, and the pairings of huge fountain-shaped grasses with paddle-leaved cannas, sinuous yuccas, and billowing, thundercloud shrubs make for a sumptuous view that changes from each fresh perspective.

Before committing anything to the ground, group all the plants you are planning to use in a given bed. If you don't have enough contrasting shapes to work with, go back to the nursery and collect an armload of site-suitable plants that offer a wider range of contours. Back home, just move those pots about, trying each plant with several others until the result dazzles your eye. Spikes and spears pair readily with rounded mounds and silky sprawlers. Geometrically trim plants often combine pleasingly with shaggy or quirky ones, while fluffy, indeterminate plants that are lost on their own can safely surround those with bolder shapes. Similarly, foliage sizes, shapes, textures, and colors are contrasted to create a running weave of leaf patterns, whether potent or subtle, which are supportive of but not dependent upon flowers. Flowers do indeed influence naturalistic composition, especially in colorist borders, where they are placed not just to produce a blurry smear of a given color at a given season, but to emphasize and echo other colors and shapes around them.

This kind of interrelated, multidimensional composition is enormous fun to play with, and surprisingly easy to contrive once the basic principles are grasped. Indeed, many people who have been frustrated by the subtleties of purely colorist placement challenges find architectural plantings a snap. When your eye becomes trained to see plants as much in terms of shape as color, it's easy to edit an unsatisfactory grouping. (If it seems as if you are always editing, that's because you are. Editing is an ongoing process, and one that alters with time and your own changing taste.)

To test the idea, walk out to the garden and look over an unsatisfactory section of a bed or border. Try to analyze it in terms of shape and form, and you'll start to pinpoint areas of difficulty almost immediately. Too many shapeless plants together will cry out for sharp contrasts. A group with too many strong characters will obviously look more restful if a few softer ones are interjected for visual relief. An excess of cascaders can look sorrowful, but some determined uprights will set them off excitingly. Beds with too many uprights will look stretched and restless, but an infusion of soothing mounds and sprawlers will anchor them firmly to the earth. This shape-analysis technique really works, anywhere, for any

Contrasts of form create rhythmic repeats in this long, flowing border, in that the plants foam like water over partially submerged rocks. Blue catmints (*Nepeta* species) and sages (*Salvia* species) echo the out-thrusting lines of dwarf conifers beyond pink puddles of western evening primrose, *Oenothera speciosa* 'Rosea' (formerly *O. berlandierii*) and smoky pink opium poppies (*Papaver somniferum*). Madrona garden, designed by Michael Schultz & Geoff Beasley, Sherwood, Oregon.

Autumn brings rich waves of warm color to mixed natural-istic borders, where many of the inhabitants boast mul-tiple seasons of glory. Here, a blazing red clump of *Hypericum* x *inodorum* 'Elstead' heightens the heat of the last few tufts of bee balm *(Monarda didyma)*, their tints echoed by the smoldering purple-red of its cousin, shrubby *Hypericum androsaemum* 'Albury Purple', in the background. Garden of Elizabeth Lair, Eugene, Oregon.

style. Even those bump-and-hump borders left by the builders can be enormously improved by the addition of some strong verticals, a few spreading fans, and some frothy tumblers.

Plant placement is clearly a vital key to both suc-cessful layering and extension of visual interest. Unfortu-nately, few books exist that can steer us toward optimal placement and grouping. Fortunately, we can consult those natural habitat models, which are often apt guides toward good garden practice. Looking back to that quin-tessential woodland beside the open meadow, we can see that each grouping seemed designed not just to strut its own stuff but also to support its neighbors. In the garden this ideal relationship is recreated through balanced plant proportions, which means not only that each plant is placed to advantage, but also that there is enough of each kind of plant for the grouping to read well across a dis-tance, yet not so much that the eye becomes bored. The woodland community also offers its inhabitants snug quarters without crowding. Most plants are as communal as people, preferring good company to splendid isolation. However, even thicketers need enough room to express themselves, and overcrowding invariably leads to prob-lems in plant or human communities. Taking another tip from the woods, we can make sure each plant and group receives and is allowed to keep its own chunk of the border. Part of the garden editing job is maintaining boundaries, making sure that no plant is thriving at another's expense.

The communal nature of plants is what makes planned communities as successful as natural ones. Like those friendly woodlanders, garden-adaptive plants get along well with others, sharing root space and nutritional resources without sulking. Adaptive, cooperative plants prosper in gardens without demanding more than their share of resources or requiring too much attention from the gardener. What we are trying to do is recreate the kind of intentional community that nature made in the woods. Selecting cooperators over prima donnas will forward our cause tremendously.

Again, we can take our cues from natural plant communities. For example, in the Pacific Northwest, monkey flowers *(Mimulus* species*)* abound. Some can be found only in very specific kinds of settings, such as rocky streambanks with excellent drainage and constant moisture in perfect balance. Others can be found in dozens of habitats, sunny and shady, damp and dry. These last can be successfully persuaded to grow in gardens, and plenty of pretty forms have been selected and named. Conversely, those stream dwellers nearly always fail in captivity, unable to make the transition into the border. This is indeed a good rule of thumb to consider when looking for garden-worthy and garden-compatible plants among the native flora. Those few plants that do prefer solitude are rarely adaptable enough to make happy garden plants.

Choosing Plants Wisely

The best performers are cooperators, so it makes sense to make sure that a majority of the garden plants we choose are site-adaptive and easygoing. That's a sound place to start, but other considerations apply as well. When we select key woody plants that even in maturity will not exceed the size and shape our design requires, we eliminate a great deal of control-oriented repetitive work (such

as hard pruning). This doesn't mean that the gardener will never be called on to prune plants; this, too, is editing, and as such is an ongoing and deeply important part of layered garden making.

Choosing wisely also means that, wherever possible, we replace poor plant choices—choices that create extra work for us—with better ones. Ideal plant choices produce what we want for and from our gardens. The ideal rarely occurs in gardens—or anywhere else—but fortunately, even less than ideal choices can transform control-oriented gardening into a more cooperative venture. When we are working with our plants, we can harness the natural forces that shape them. When we set ourselves up to work against our plants, we are caught in a dominating relationship where our plants are inevitably trying desperately to do what we don't want them to, and we are forced to constantly frustrate their natural inclinations. Clearly, the more we know about our plants and about their likely performance under the specific conditions we can offer them, the more smoothly our designed community is apt to function, both esthetically and in terms of plant health.

Delighting Eye and Spirit

Becoming a well-educated plant person will involve visiting as many gardens and nurseries as possible, studying the ways in which plants we want to grow respond to local conditions. General-purpose garden books are excellent guides, but none can help as much as touring regional gardens. For one thing, it's quite difficult to envision how a plant—especially a woody one—will appear when fully grown. Mature trees and shrubs can often be seen in parks, arboreta, and zoos, as well as in public and private gardens. It's quite a surprise to see what happens to a sapling over time. Nursery labels are not always good indicators of a plant's size at maturity, because the nursery trade recognizes a sad truth—most of the woody plants sold from garden centers will be dead within two to five years. The height found on a nursery label is often just the plant's probable height at ten years (the average life span of survivors). Seeing well-grown plants and finding out how old they are (when possible) will give you a good idea of how much space to allow your woody plants in your own beds and borders.

Unfortunately, when you get your young trees and shrubs home from the nursery and set them out at the proper distances apart, the dark side of this excellent planting practice will immediately be apparent. The beds look empty and the plants look lonely. I once saw a home border laid out by a well-intentioned gardener who not only did his research faithfully but also used a yardstick to aid his placement. Since the woody plants were mostly quite young and small, the result looked like a bad party where nobody brought any wine and all the guests wandered aimlessly around, never connecting with the others.

It is worth stating here that a cardinal rule of planting is to create a strong sense of generosity and abundance. Among English border makers, it is considered a horticultural crime to allow any bare soil to show between plants after the middle of May. To avoid the appearance of stingy planting, we can fill in those gaping holes with annuals and easily moved perennials. Year One, these mixed plantings will appear pleasingly plump. Year Two, both the woody plants and the perennials will have bulked out, but

by eliminating the annuals there will still be plenty of room. Year Three, everything will look terrific, but by Year Four, it will be time to reposition those place-holding perennials, dividing the big clumps and moving them elsewhere. Within five years a well-planned garden made even with very young and small woody components will look convincingly mature.

As in any planting system, larger things will be congregated at the back of borders and beds, but in naturalistically layered gardens, taller plants may also be introduced throughout them since the object is to create a more natural-looking topography. An eye-catchingly irregular topography is created almost automatically when our plantings emphasize form. Most traditional borders have the topography of a bread loaf, largely because the multidimensionality of plants is not stressed. From most viewing angles, typical colorist borders have the bosomy outline of a rolltop desk. The individual plants merge into the whole. In contrast, when taller plants are placed amid somewhat shorter ones, they emerge like living sculpture. "Sculptural" means much the same thing in plants as in any other medium: If the basic shape of the plant is taken to mean its silhouette or outline against the skyline, then its sculptural

---

This young garden is just a year old, but already the array of textures and forms weaves distinctive patterns in these naturalistic mixed borders. Rough rock walls break the steep slope into two planting areas. Behind, towering native trees give the small garden a majestic skyline, requiring the design to employ more boldness of scale than such narrow borders might otherwise suggest. Lovejoy/Rogers garden, Bainbridge Island, Washington.

form is that shape with depth and mass. Certain plants, such as large hostas, Siberian iris, and yuccas, are obviously sculptural, but others may require thoughtful placement to make their multidimensionality apparent.

Successful placement creates a marvelous visual flow, filling our planting beds full of treats and surprises. As you stroll past them in one direction, a series of ever-altering vignettes present themselves to your eye. Make the return trip in the opposite direction, and new relationships and partnerings will be revealed. This is not the traditional "billowing border," shapeless as a Mother Hubbard dress; the plantings will have structural strength and architectural appeal, and individual plants will play the role of sculpture, becoming garden art in their own right.

Left: Sinuous madrona trunks stand storklike amid a flurry of spring bulbs and early perennials. Madronas resent root disturbance and are not pleased to have quantities of shrubs clustered around their knees, so care must be taken to leave these beautiful native trees plenty of elbowroom. Low, ruffled plantings of airy shrubs and shallow-rooted perennials accompany these trees in natural settings, and may safely be emulated in gardens as well. Garden of Cyril Hume, Sidney, British Columbia.

Right: Native garry or white oaks, *Quercus garryana*, dancing in the woods. Their joyful lines carry over into gardens where they are treated as welcome guests. To keep them happy in captivity, avoid excessive summer watering and give them room to express their character without crowding.

Northwest Naturalistic

Northwest Naturalistic

chapter 3

The union of mild climate, remarkable native flora, and multicultural influences has given the coastal Northwest a certain edge when it comes to developing new styles of garden design. Informally shaped and deeply layered, many gardens depart from more traditional styles by being plant-centered, celebrating the natural shapes of the floral components, and frankly emulating the ragged-edged, often irregular tiers of nature's own plantings.

Nearly all of these gardens are tucked into or edging onto woodlands. Those sites that lack the advantage of natural woods to back them up borrow freely from the neighbors. By edging their own gardens with cleverly layered hedges, made by combining small trees and large shrubs, the designers manage to enclose the garden space and provide visual privacy while also creating the illusion of a far larger, deeper garden that includes mature trees on other properties. By arranging the hedge plants to frame them, even distant trees can be incorporated into the tree line of the borrower's garden.

In the Pacific Northwest, second-growth woodlands make magnificent garden backdrops, and the elegant native understory mingles readily with ornamental exotics. Here Asian and native rhododendrons are underplanted with ferns and mosses, the beds threaded with scores of wildflowers and hybrid primulas. Sunrise Gardens, designed by Bobbie Garthwaite & Joe Sullivan, Bainbridge Island, Washington.

Although traditional hardscape elements such as patios, trellises, walls, and fences may be present within these gardens, woody plants are treated as living architecture, forming the gardens' columns and pillars, arbors and arches. Plants with pronounced eccentricity of line are especially prized and given companions that underline their individuality. Specimen shrubs and small trees are

The saturated green of coastal Cascadia gives naturalistic gardens a glowing presence in every season. In winter, each sculptural stump and log bears a thick, velvety coat of moss. The native mosses bloom during the cold months, when their color is particularly brilliant and their luxuriant qualities are most apparent. Sunrise Gardens, designed by Bobbie Garthwaite & Joe Sullivan, Bainbridge Island, Washington.

used sculpturally, placed like pieces of art to function as centerpieces for borders and beds. Indeed, where mature plantings are being edited and reshaped to this end, the beds will be formed around existing character plants, for the design of these gardens is soundly plant driven.

Paths are almost never straight, but wind between existing trees and shrubs, curving here to avoid a low branch or veering there in order to present a better view of a moss-covered stump or a huge and intricately shaped tree root. Rather than attempting to even out a site, naturalistic design makes much of any change of grade, finding opportunities to create overlooks both large and small. Some viewpoints offer vistas of the garden as a whole, while others give only glimpses that focus the attention on tiny, intimate vignettes, creating the sense of a secret garden within the garden.

This young style developed initially in the region known to geographers and gardeners as Cascadia. Stretching from British Columbia to Northern California, Cascadia is bound by mountains to the east and the sea to the west, encompassing the mild, coastal areas of the Pacific Northwest. Blessed with short, mild winters, Cascadia is a

Naturalistic gardens echo and amplify the patterns and partnerships of the native flora, repeating the lines and massing of the natural understory. Trees and shrubs are set like sculptural elements within the beds, which pour seamlessly into native plantings behind them. Where gardens merge with wild woods, as here, these transition areas become especially important. Sunrise Gardens, designed by Bobbie Garthwaite & Joe Sullivan, Bainbridge Island, Washington.

land where year-round gardens can alter with the seasons, retaining their character and presence even in winter. Given the climate and the native flora, it is not particularly surprising that this region should give rise to gardens that stretch the garden year, since its gardeners have every possible encouragement (including some of the country's finest nurseries) to seek to extend their gardens' glory from earliest spring through the deep of winter.

Naturalistic Fusion

Among the most fascinating of the Northwestern naturalistic gardens are those that take cues from natural surroundings, then amplify them, combining the abundance of the English herbaceous border with the artist's spatial sensibility. This group of gardens owes a strong debt to plant placement patterns seen in Asian gardens, especially Zen tea and sand gardens, both of which emphasize the spare and the sculptural. In general, the naturalistic designers are less apt to employ the lean look of the Zen gardens, but instead allow that sensibility to temper the English abundance. In their gardens, plantings tend to be strongly sculptural, each component placed with thoughtful assessment of its physical characteristics and a profound appreciation for its architectural qualities. Most

Naturalistic gardens often favor Asian models that stress the shapes of plants and the negative space between the plants. Alternating open areas with densely planted ones makes for a fascinating interplay of light and shadow, clean lines, and solid masses. Portland Japanese Garden, Portland, Oregon.

of these gardens do celebrate plants in profusion, spilling over with floral riches, yet the wealth of plant material is not permitted to blend into a blur of color. Each combination, vignette, and composition is dominated by the potent lines of the individual plants involved. Rather than being perennial-based, like so many famous English gardens, these combine perennials with lively mixtures of garden-worthy natives and trees, shrubs, vines, and bulbs imported from similar climate zones all over the world.

In design, these naturalistic gardens refer repeatedly to their natural surroundings, whether directly or through the borrowed views that draw in trees and large plants that can be seen from the garden. However, just as the plant palette extends beyond the local flora, their designs are not limited to the attempted recreation of natural patterns. Unlike habitat or "natural" gardens, the new naturalistic gardens first incorporate, then stretch past the givens of the natural environment, adapting and incorporating suitable design elements from a myriad of traditional styles, combining them with both sensitivity and a playful experimentation.

Until quite recently, it was standard practice for landscape architects and garden designers to recommend that homeowners remove all or most native plants before beginning a new garden. Ten years ago, close to a dozen professional designers suggested the same thing when I was preparing to make a large garden in an area bordering on deep woods. Nearly all advised further that it would be far easier to see what we had to work with once the visual distractions of the native plants were removed. Today—in the coastal Northwest, at any rate—far fewer designers would take that rejecting approach or suggest the exclusive use of imported plants. This represents a

At Sunrise Gardens, sweet woodruff (Galium odoratum) and Welsh poppies (Meconopsis cambrica) spread in colorful, scented carpets beneath wild and garden rhododendrons, maples, and flowering cherries. Native lady ferns punctuate the plantings, while wild wood violets, sandworts (Arenaria species) and mosses clothe the flowing green paths. Sunrise Gardens, designed by Bobbie Garthwaite & Joe Sullivan, Bainbridge Island, Washington.

cultural shift in vision, one which more deeply respects the environment and reflects a consciousness of our altering relationship with the natural world and our immediate surroundings.

Emulating the Layers of Nature

My morning car pool takes me past not just my favorite woodland but a whole variety of settings, from dense woods to open meadows, through a small village and into the suburbs. Though the plants and plantings vary greatly in each habitat, the essential relationships between them remain fairly constant. Perhaps the best place to see the overall patterns is along the edge of that open meadow I described earlier, where mature woodland has been cut away to make fields for a local farmer. There, the deep woods are full of mixed trees, deciduous and evergreen. In winter, their shapes create striking visual patterns, rich with detail.

On the largest scale, the open, spreading canopies of bigleaf and vine maples alternate with round-headed cascaras and the elongated ovals of alders and willows. Mature Douglas firs soar above them, spirelike in form, their great branches shaggy and drooping low to the ground. Cedars present a tighter profile and finer texture, though they, too, are firmly upright in form, while full-skirted hemlocks dip their bobbing tips as if unsure of their final direction. Upright, linear alders punctuate the dark, heavy mass of evergreens with slim, silvery verticals. The understory combines thicketing redtwig dogwoods with wiry, emerald green Scotch broom, delicately textured huckleberries, and solid lumps of salal (Gaultheria shallon). Repeated contrasts of form and texture set off the occasional eccentric shape—usually a locust tree—with striking clarity. The result is harmonious, rhythmic, subtle, comforting to eye and spirit in every light, weather, or season.

Naturalistic designers model their gardens upon nature, arranging their plants in similarly comfortable-looking communities based on the plants' shared cultural requirements. Many strictly "natural" gardens employ only native plants and attempt to recreate habitat. Most are more earnest than beautiful, and for many years, artful garden makers looked askance at the natural movement, finding it unnecessarily limited in palette and intention. The Northwesterners making these new naturalistic borders are expanding that viewpoint dramatically. They have recognized that naturalistic placement does not preclude artful plant combinations. Indeed, if the point is not only to integrate plants effectively in terms of color, form, and texture, but to underline their inherent sculptural qualities and minimize any flaws of form or weaknesses of line, then success in this endeavor is nothing short of a high art form.

Layering plants in naturalistic garden settings is based on comparable principles. Plants are given a site and setting that suits their requirements. They are given enough room to achieve their potential size, mass, and form. They are surrounded with compatible companions, all of which enjoy similar conditions. Finally, they are set in physical relationships to each other that emphasize the sculptural qualities of each plant. This is really a matter of looking and paying attention. What sets a sculpture apart from, say, a painting is its multiple dimensions. Plants are not flat. They have mass and depth as well as height and width. Because height and width are the only features that are apparent on a planting diagram or picture, it is easy to

forget the 3-D quality of plants, but unless it is taken fully into account, it is very hard to integrate woody and ephemeral plants into a lastingly coherent design.

Paying attention to the specifics of each woody plant in particular—what this particular specimen really looks like—will drive its placement and its relationship to companions. Nearly all designers create plans for planting, but the best of them plant from real life, guided by the actual plants they are placing rather than by theoretical drawings created at a desk. Ideally, they are also guided by what's already there. It's very easy to spot gardens that have been transferred from paper to earth without taking this into consideration: There are few if any transitions between the old plantings and the new. The eye seeks in vain for links between the artificial and the natural, and we end up unconsciously trying to edit out the backdrop, rather than being assisted to integrate it into the garden. Whether the overall goal is simply to create an ornamental garden with a natural feel, to maintain or reestablish habitat, or to transition the garden seamlessly into wild areas, the same underlying guidelines must be observed. In the new naturalistic gardens, we see precisely how plants can be woven together in relational patterns that evoke the natural and awaken in the viewer a sense that the garden is connected to its place.

Quintessential Naturalism

The quintessential Northwestern naturalistic garden is a recently resuscitated nursery garden near my home. Decades ago, Sunrise Nursery was a mecca for rhododendron lovers. Sited on the edge of mature woodlands, the nursery was threaded by a small stream and filled with an

abundance of woodland wildflowers. After many years of utter neglect, the elderly garden was a ruin. Seven years ago it was bought by Bobbie Garthwaite and Joe Sullivan, who patiently labored to bring it back to life. Rather than clearing away the often unsightly old plants, they tended them with care, mulching and feeding before slowly beginning a restorative pruning process. Although rhododendrons are resilient, and hard-pruning them to stumps can result in a strong flush of new growth, the couple wanted to preserve the character and dignity of the seasoned, venerable plants.

This thoughtful approach did not work in every instance, but it was successful in enough cases that the garden today has the feeling of a thriving community in that plants of all ages are growing together. In many areas, new beds are being built up around long-established plants that lend instant presence to the new plantings. The intermediate-sized shrubs and perennials brought into these new beds serve several purposes, underlining the maturity of the garden, uniting the tree line and upper story of the woods with the smaller plants, and gently carrying the eye back down to the more intimate scale of the garden. At ground level, the younger plants are clustered around these grande dames, much as queenly mother plants in natural

In a remarkable example of self-healing, this mossy primula bed knit itself in an open area where an old shed, junked cars, and a lifetime collection of beer bottles had once accumulated. Bobbie has thinned the volunteers, and is also introducing a number of minor bulbs to the enchanting scene. Sunrise Gardens, designed by Bobbie Garthwaite & Joe Sullivan, Bainbridge Island, Washington.

colonies have smaller satellites around their skirts.

This pattern echoes a planting technique characteristic of naturalistic gardens, where the designer will position a striking small tree or specimen shrub as a centerpiece for a bed or border, surrounding it with secondary and tertiary plantings that underline its most decorative attributes. When care is taken in the selection of these subsidiary plants, they can continue to support the central, sculptural plant in every season, whether through beauty of line and form or with evergreen bulk and mass.

Like colorist gardens, naturalistic borders may have an overall theme, often based on the character of the central plant, and each section of a large border may similarly develop its own subtheme. Key character plants become focal points for their own beds, and significant vignettes are built up around these dominant central forms. At Sunrise Gardens, a flowering cherry, a Japanese maple, a viburnum, or a star magnolia might take center stage, abundantly underplanted with running carpets of sweet violets, native foam flower (*Tiarella trifoliata*), false Solomon's seal (*Smilacina racemosa*), and coral bells (*Heuchera cylindrica*). Natives mingle happily with garden plants of similar constitution and habits, knitting into solid carpets that eventually become all but impenetrable by unwanted weeds.

There are few barren areas, since dozens of willing runners and creepers, native and exotic, were allowed to spread freely over the years. Bobbie very quickly began editing enthusiastic volunteers such as Welsh poppy (*Meconopsis cambrica*), sweet woodruff, and several kinds of bishop's hat (*Epimedium* species), thinning and mulching worn-out colonies and replanting fresh divisions where less desirable plants deserved replacement.

Old-fashioned primroses began to appear as she cleared ground around the overgrown beds, and she introduced a series of candelabra primulas that have also proliferated generously. Sheets of minor bulbs—crocus, scilla, and grape hyacinths—are multiplying rapidly, as well as the native trilliums and dogtooth violets (*Erythronium revolutum*). Throughout the year, successive waves of color wash over and through the beds. As Bobbie edits the waves, the matrix that produces these sheets of living color becomes increasingly better balanced, its components ever more compatible. This is vital, since in order for lastingly harmonious relationships to be achieved, such densely interplanted layers must cooperate extensively both under and above ground.

A sturdy backbone of native plants gives Sunrise Gardens a continual flow of life and change. Even in the depths of winter, the garden glows with verdant moss and tender, celadon-green lichens that trim the branches of twiggy shrubs and trees like frilly little flowers. The sculptural trunks and enormous root balls of fallen trees have been left to molder undisturbed. Thickly crusted over with mosses and mushrooms, those in more advanced stages of decay become nurse logs, nourishing succeeding crops of sword and licorice ferns (*Polystichum munitum* and *Polypodium glycyrrhiza*, respectively), huckleberries (*Vaccinium ovatum*), and glossy salal (*Gaultheria shallon*). Eventually, shrubs and trees rise up along the run of the trunk, replacing the fallen giant with eager saplings that leap up to the light let in by the mother tree's removal from the canopy.

In one area of this garden, a magical piece of self-healing has taken place over several years. After masses of old bottles, car parts, and the ruins of a junk shed were removed, a large flat area was opened up between the house and the stream bank. While Bobbie was still trying to figure out what to do with it, this garden-within-the-garden sheeted itself over with mosses and began sprouting hundreds of candelabra primulas. Now the initial volunteers share ground space with bulbous iris, daffodils, and violets, as well as the golden glowing native skunk cabbages (*Lysichitum americanum*).

Harnessing Natives

Grown as border beauties in England, skunk cabbages are less common in North American gardens, but their marvelous foliage and handsome, hooded flowers surely earn them a solid spot in any border planted for line and form. At Sunrise Gardens, these bog lilies (as the English so euphoniously call them) line the further bank of the little stream, where they are tightly interlayered with tall, lacy lady ferns (*Athyrium filix-femina*) and dramatically linear horsetails, or scouring rush (*Equisetum hyemale*). Dreaded by gardeners, horsetails are much sought-after by flower arrangers, who prize their bold lines and delicate texture.

Winter rain and runoff pours through the narrow streambed, raising it far above summer levels. Streamside plants need careful anchoring if they are not to be washed away, and preference is given to natives with sturdy, erosion-resistant root systems like skunk cabbages, lady ferns, and even horsetails. Hybrid primulas also do surprisingly well here, despite the flux and flow of high water. Sunrise Gardens, designed by Bobbie Garthwaite & Joe Sullivan, Bainbridge Island, Washington.

The dense native understory readily accommodates fine-textured azaleas and larger-leaved rhododendrons, as well as colonizing hardy geraniums, hostas, and hellebores. In deep woods like this, most of the lower branches on the tallest firs are already dead and wind snapped, but close pruning of the stumps exposes their clean, strong lines and turns the trunks into living columns. Weesjes garden, Sidney, British Columbia.

This scouring rush is less invasive than other species of horsetail, and its spread can be controlled by raising the pH of the acid native soils nearer to neutral (the rush prefers strongly acid soils). This pH trick is most easily achieved through frequent (as in several times each year) applications of buffering compost and aged manure, both of which are nearly pH neutral.

The small natural stream that now dominates the garden was nearly lost to weeds and sludge when Bobbie and Joe first bought the garden. They spent several seasons dredging its mucky bed, dumping the rich but stinky spoils in the compost heap to enrich impoverished parts of the garden. When they finally exposed sound bottom, they brought in gravel to line it, but heavy winter rains have scoured out the channel so thoroughly that little gravel is now left. Each year, when the spring rains cease, they remove more viscous heaps of excess soil, having learned that only by keeping the stream's course fairly clear can they avoid losing a great many plants, which otherwise wash away during winter floods. In winter and spring the water is in full spate, roaring through the garden and frequently overflowing the narrow streambed. In several areas, Joe finally built baffles to slow down the flood and retain bedside plantings.

By summer the stream has dwindled to a quiet trickle. The small pool Joe and Bobbie created looks soothingly meditative, reflecting blossom and sky. It's hard to remember then that in just a few months, this gentle stream will be a serious force once again. The densely planted banks are now secured by a weaving of candelabra primulas and bog iris with native skunk cabbage, horsetails, and lady ferns, all excellent bank holders. Editing, however, is a constant process wherever woods and garden meet.

This discovery is shared by many other gardeners who strive to wed woodlands with cultivated areas. In most cases the transition zones between the garden proper and the wild are the weakest in design and planting. Perhaps the most graceful way to deal with this tricky matter is simply to allow smoother transitions to form themselves. By selectively permitting native plants to insert themselves into the fringes of our designs, and by letting natural plantings influence our artificial ones, we make those critical visual links that create comfort by emphasizing similarities. Editing the woods beyond our garden space, eliminating clutter and crowding, will further unite the two areas by revealing natural graces of form and making the complex interplay of plants more readily visible.

A Naturalistic Collector's Garden

On Vancouver Island in British Columbia, Canada, two botanists, Nick and Evelyn Weesjes, have made an exceptional naturalistic collector's garden that houses hundreds of species and hybrid rhododendrons amid mature woods. For over twenty years they spent every free weekend clearing paths and trails, creating planting beds, and thinning the forest understory to make room for their enormous collection of plants. Early on they determined to preserve as much as possible of the native flora, respecting its natural beauty, as much as they loved the look of their rhododendrons. Now both gardeners are retired, and although the bulk of the garden is well established, they spend most of every day in the 20-acre garden, grooming and editing to maintain a harmonious balance.

The Weesjes' garden meanders gracefully through the woods, its paths directed as much by gigantic trees and

Native wood sorrel, *Oxalis oregana*, comes in several forms, with pink or white flowers and evergreen foliage backed by bronzed red undersides. Here a bank of mixed ground covers has lost the battle for supremacy with the finest of local sorrel variants, a form selected years ago for vigor and year-round good looks. Weesjes garden, Sidney, British Columbia.

handsome shrubs as by any human desire to "get some-place." Scores of powerful plant pictures present them-selves as you stroll the paths, marveling at the myriad ways in which native plants have interwoven with introduced ones. Over the years many imported plants have sown themselves thickly into the forest floor. Candelabra prim-ulas follow streambeds, as both seeds and young plants were washed along by winter floods. Ferns and mosses cover every fallen log, natives mingling happily with exotics. Introduced ground covers merge with masses of native wood sorrel *(Oxalis oregana)* that, assisted initially by Evelyn and Nick, now pour in thick green blankets over banks and slopes.

Now mature, the vast rhododendron collection requires only minor pruning to keep plants in good trim and to repair damage after winter storms. Some of these are arboreal, soaring to join the evergreen madronas *(Arbutus menziesii)*, Douglas firs *(Pseudotsuga menziesii)*, and bigleaf maples *(Acer macrophyllum)*. Others make bulky, sculptural masses between airy huckleberries and bushy Indian plum *(Oemleria cerasiformis)*.

Though the ornamental plantings were installed over several decades, the result is amazingly coherent,

largely because the point and purpose of the original design was never forgotten. Each rhododendron was placed for plant health and optimal viewing, and all the rest is supportive. During the long creative process, the Weesjes never lost sight of where they were headed. Their respectful, appreciative approach to gardening within the woods made it possible to preserve the authentic quality of those woods and allow plenty of room for native plants to develop and spread as is their wont, while at the same time incorporating hundreds of specimen plants in a natural-looking manner.

Ironically, now that the Weesjes have retired, the task of keeping the enormous garden tidy and thriving fills their days. Slowly but steadily, they move through the grounds, tempering nature's tendency toward chaos. Ratty evergreen ferns are cut to the ground each year; excess seedlings are thinned and moved; and established colonies are adjusted in size for health and well-being. Though most natural litter is allowed to remain in place to form nature's own compost, larger leaves are carefully removed from smaller plants, while broken branches and blown-off limbs are periodically gathered up. A large shredder con-verts them to coarse chips, which are recycled back into garden paths. Judicious pruning exposes the clean natural shapes of shrubs and trees and keeps maturing plants in proper trim. Fortunately, as Evelyn observes, the work is far from thankless. Tending such a community, a hybrid between the natural and the artificial, and seeing the potency and beauty in its success is rewarding indeed. The garden continues to be a joy in itself and an ongoing gift for others, whose responses are also rewarding gifts to these generous garden makers.

Sculptural placement results in effortlessly handsome plantings like this one, where ferns, hostas, and primulas are effectively backed with shapely evergreen rhododen-drons, twiggy native dogwoods, and willows. Annual editing and light pruning keep these cooperative plantings in good trim, while deep mulches recycled from fallen limbs and branches keep them free of weeds. Weesjes garden, Sidney, British Columbia.

PLANT PORTRAIT

Flowering Currant, *Ribes sanguineum*

From March into June, rosy red currant, *Ribes sanguineum* (Zone 5, 6'–12'), brightens woods, meadows, and gardens throughout the Northwest. The floral show is prolonged because the blossoms, which dangle in long clusters, open sequentially. The flowers are followed by fat, bright blue berries (edible but not very tasty) that show to advantage against the clear gold of the autumn foliage.

A willing worker with a pleasingly casual shape, red currant fits into woodsy settings and informal shade gardens. Its small pleated leaves open into little tri-lobed fans with a toothed and scalloped edge. In the wild this shrub is bushy and upright, stretching as much as 10 to 12 feet high. Named garden forms are shorter (4'–8') and shapelier, and most are notable for heavy bloom.

Wild plants mostly flower in warm shades of pink that attract hungry hummingbirds. Numerous colorful forms have been named over the years, both here and in England. Ruddy 'King Edward VII' is one of the richest reds, while vivid 'Pulborough Scarlet' is the deepest. A variegated form of this last, with yellow-edged foliage, may occasionally be found in specialty nurseries. Clear, medium-pink 'Claremont' ages to soft red, blending well with rosy rhododendrons and purple azaleas. The silvery pink panicles of 'Spring Showers' are elegantly elongated, reaching 6 to 8 inches in mature plants. Delicate, pale 'Pokey's Pink' fits into the tenderest pastel schemes, as do creamy 'Hannaman White', crisp 'Spring Snow', and long-panicled, large-flowered 'White Icicle'.

Native red currant, *Ribes sanguineum*, comes in a number of excellent color forms. All bloom early in the year, when their flashy flowers make a cheerful splash in the damp green garden. Ribes root quickly from cuttings, and can be grown for years in containers while the gardener decides exactly where this willing shrub really ought to be placed. Garden of Ernie & Marietta O'Byrne, Eugene, Oregon.

PLANT PORTRAIT

Skunk Cabbage, *Lysichitum americanum*

This glorious denizen of western bogs makes a surprisingly good garden plant. Despite the common name, neither leaves nor flowers of skunk cabbage are in the least bit stinky unless they are bruised or broken, which is entirely avoidable. In fact, the great, hooded flowers have a faintly sweet, wild honey scent, most readily discernible on still, warm spring days. Flower arranger Barry Ferguson showed me that by standing cut skunk cabbages (which, like broken ones, do exude that pungent namesake scent) in a bucket of warm water for a few hours, all trace of the skunky odor will be gone, and the flowers can be used to grace a table indoors without any suggestion of unpleasant smell.

Young plants grown from seed are very easy to transplant into beds and borders, where they will grow quickly, given decent soil and average water. They grow especially well in damp areas, and are an ideal border filler for persistently wet spots. Give them plenty of room, however, because these lovely creatures get very large, in time stretching a good 4 feet across and rising a yard high. Not surprisingly, the root system that supports such vigorous growth is correspondingly large. Mature plants are all but impossible to move, for the thick roots plunge endlessly into the earth.

Skunk cabbage, or bog lily, is a strikingly architectural plant, from the time the tight sheaves thrust through the ground until midsummer, when the great, cabbage-like leaves go dormant. They appreciate mucky, boggy ground, but also grow well in borders. Sunrise Gardens, designed by Bobbie Garthwaite & Joe Sullivan, Bainbridge Island, Washington.

Stroll Gardens

Stroll Gardens

chapter 4

Northwestern stroll gardens are fusion gardens, wedding elements drawn from Asian and English landscape traditions. Serene in atmosphere, clean in line, they are full of architectural plants artfully and often sculpturally arrayed. Some stroll gardens have the elegance of simplicity, achieving their powerful visual effects with just a few kinds of well-chosen plants. Many are collector's gardens, brilliantly incorporating a tremendously broad plant palette without succumbing to visual chaos. Urban, suburban, or rural, these meditative retreats are also thriving plant communities that adapt comfortably to a wide range of settings and conditions. All of these gardens are characterized by loosely layered, naturalistic planting arrangements that accentuate the graceful, potent natural shapes of important plants, notably specimen trees.

Traditional Japanese stroll gardens are designed so that various aspects of the gardens' many vistas and vignettes present themselves to visitors as they walk the wandering paths. The element of surprise is created through screening, blocking off parts of the garden with

In traditional Japanese tea gardens, even minor changes of grade are emphasized to create overlooks and inner vistas. Plants are placed with an eye to their sculptural qualities, and paths are cleverly laid out to give the illusion of greater depth and length to the garden. Portland Japanese Garden, Portland, Oregon.

interlayered groups of trees and shrubs. It is further achieved by making paths that wind gently, enticing the viewer onward to see what comes next, rather than running arrow straight, as in geometrically based European designs that often expose large parts of the garden to view all at once. Even where actual space is very limited, this path-curving technique can be successfully adapted, lending a sense of mystery and creating an impression of visual extension, both of which are often lacking in tiny gardens.

In a few classic stroll gardens, such as the Detached Palace (Rikyu) in Kyoto, straight lines are used in certain areas as a deliberate conceit, intended to underline the contrast between the naturalistic plantings and the artificiality of the linear elements. Generally, however, straight lines and severe axes are avoided as too jarringly unnatural.

Many Japanese stroll gardens are made within spacious pleasure grounds, where wide paths lead the ambler from water to woods and from open, sunny parks to shady dells. At each turn, natural objects—often stones—and artificial objects, such as sculptured stone lanterns, are placed to capture the eye and intrigue the viewer. Woody plants, often combined with low shrubs, and occasionally with perennials of various kinds, are arrayed in natural-looking groupings. These groups and clusters are interrupted at frequent intervals, chiefly by water features such as lakes, ponds, and rushing streams.

Changes of grade are very often incorporated to create waterfalls and cascades, as well as outlooks and overviews. Large-scale plantings of trees and shrubs are placed where they most effectively break up territorial views. As one walks, tantalizing glimpses of broader views are periodically presented to the eye, framed by cleverly placed ever-greens and sinuous tree trunks. Finally, the meandering path emerges at an overlook point, a place where the greater landscape, and perhaps vistas that extend far beyond it, will be more fully revealed. The clustered plantings that line the paths also serve to screen and frame interior views, alternately baffling and rewarding the traveling viewer in the same way that changes of grade create changes of viewpoint.

Modern Japanese stroll gardens, such as Ritsurin found in Takamatsu City, often have the flavor of an English park. This seems surprising at first, yet the idea of a reverse East/West fusion is not so unlikely after all. Although the Victorian craze for the Japanesque is well documented, less has been written about the opposite influence, although it certainly existed. Indeed, many contemporary Japanese gardeners are feverishly recreating English herbaceous borders for clamoring clients. There are more new members of the Hardy Plant Society in Japan than anywhere else in the world. This fad seems tragic to those who worry that traditional Japanese gardens will be lost. Perhaps, however, it will lead to the development of still more fusion gardens, and to design concepts that we can't yet imagine.

Water-rounded rocks cluster along the wide, bark-chip paths, suggesting stones along a riverbank or sea wrack on a wave-washed beach. The gently curving paths lead eye and foot alike, drawing the stroller ever onward. Though actual distances may be quite short, the illusion of longer vistas is supported by the loosely layered plantings, which blur path edges and hide the path's end. Garden of Robin Hopper & Judi Dyelle, Metchosin, British Columbia.

Certain Zen gardens can also be seen as stroll gardens, in that visitors journey along a path that transports them away from the mundane world and leads them inward. Zen gardens are designed to nourish the spirit, encouraging a meditative, reflective state in those who venture therein. The intention is to heighten human awareness of our interconnectedness with the natural world. Interestingly, despite the fact that many Zen garden design elements appear utterly artificial to Western eyes, they nearly always function precisely as they are meant to, whether or not untrained viewers understand their symbolic meanings. Most of us come away from such gardens refreshed by the reminder that the connection between man and nature is as much spiritual as physical.

In the United States, ideas similar to those that inform classic Japanese and Chinese garden design were propounded some fifty years ago through the work of several landscape architects, including James Rose. Rose in particular found fault with the Beaux Arts influence that dominated Harvard's landscape architecture program in the 1930s. Though less publicly recognized than some of his peers, Rose's ideas profoundly affected those of classmates like Garrett Eckbo and Dan Kiley, and indirectly changed the way North Americans gardened. Rose was fascinated by Japanese Zen garden design, which deeply informs his own residential designs. Before his time very

few garden designers paid the slightest attention to the role of sound in garden design: Rose's work with the musical qualities of moving water and susurrant bamboo was revolutionary in his day and remains influential, if little acknowledged, even now. He was also among the first to bring a sculptural sensibility to plant placement and to treat negative space with as much respect as the plantings and hardscape.

Rose's appreciation for abstract sculpture and constructivist painting led him to create gardens that reflected his remarkable awareness of space, light, and texture. Most designers only know his work from photographs, if at all, yet even the pictures are powerful enough to make us rethink the common preconceptions that limit our ideas about ways in which architecture and gardenscape can be related.

Many North American stroll gardens show a Rosian influence, which is nearly always unconscious. One exception is a Canadian garden, that of the late Elizabeth England in Victoria, British Columbia. Elizabeth was a librarian and a fine researcher whose investigations into garden history and design traditions led her far beyond the usual knowledge base. Her own garden grew into its present shape over twenty years, altering as her life role changed. When her children were small, the yard served as a play place, and the garden was modest. As the children grew up, so did the garden, which now encompasses every inch of its long urban lot.

Elizabeth England was a plantswoman of fine repute, whose eye for excellent plants and sensitive placement made her an arbiter of taste for dozens of advancing garden designers. Her deep friendship with the late Kevin Nicolay of Seattle, botanical artist, garden designer, and

North American stroll gardens are often lean and simple in line, yet lush and complex in planting. The overall effect is both emotionally serene and visually stimulating, achieving a rare fusion of the meditative and the inspirational. Garden of Elizabeth England, Victoria, British Columbia.

Unlike the artless arrangements that characterize cottage gardens, these sculptural, naturalistic borders are planned to please the passerby yet provide privacy for the home. Front windows are screened with living curtains and oversized plants create a hidden bower for the gardener. Garden of Elizabeth England, Victoria, British Columbia.

plantsman extraordinaire, extended her influence far beyond her immediate neighborhood. A few years ago, English garden writer Penelope Hobhouse called Elizabeth's garden the finest small garden she had seen in Canada and greatly admired her choice of plants as well as the combinations she created. Much visited and frequently photographed, Elizabeth's garden has informed gardeners from all over the world. Slides of her garden have been seen by thousands of students who attend lectures on design and plant selection.

Elizabeth's stroll garden is a good model to explore in detail, because it is neither large nor rural. It was made without a great deal of help, and her garden budget was always modest. Despite these handicaps the garden is outstanding, rewarding multiple visits with fresh insight and discovery each time. Very simple in design, it is complex in planting, and the plants are invariably the choicest available. Though strict in her judgment, Elizabeth was not a plant snob, and she continued to grow old favorites—particularly daylilies and hostas—alongside the constant influx of new acquisitions.

The small front garden, which abuts the sidewalk, is often called a cottage garden, because its plants spill and tumble so abundantly and because the design has the casual, overflowing quality associated with cottage gardens. Elizabeth herself always pointed out (somewhat acerbically) that true cottage gardens were quite a different sort of thing. In them fruits and vegetables snuggled up to flowers of all kinds. One main path, perhaps bisected at the kitchen steps, led straight through to the outbuildings (and the privy, as often as not; thus, leading someone "up the garden path" meant giving them an unpleasant surprise). No inch of ground space was wasted,

Though this back garden is narrow, the long, meandering paths crisscross and intersect, making the available space seem surprisingly large. Trees and shrubs alternately baffle and expose interior views, disguising the amount of actual space. The tightly planted beds emphasize sculptural, high contrasts of form, employing color combinations of exquisite subtlety. Garden of Elizabeth England, Victoria, British Columbia.

and efficiency was far more important than design or color combinations.

In Elizabeth's front garden, plants and paths flow like water, wandering in and out of one another in order to create new ways to see the plants in various settings and with shifting qualities of light. Now backlit, now seen in a glitter of gold, the grasses and perennials meld into a marvelous living tapestry whose tints shift with the seasons. Near the front door, an all but hidden bench provides a novel, back-of-the-border viewpoint for the gardener, who can also enjoy the comments and responses of passersby without being seen herself.

To those passersby the sidewalk tour offers up a series of vignettes seen between trees, with tantalizing glimpses of brilliant flowers and colorful foliage for most of the year, and an enticing play of forms and textures that persists into winter. Once inside the front garden, it becomes apparent that this is a stroll garden on a miniature scale, where the wanderer must engage the imagination, descending physically or in fantasy to the level of the plants in order for them to provide enclosure. Elizabeth described this area as "a playful jungle for cats," and when you shrink your viewpoint to that of a cat, the plants draw you in to a different reality, and you leave the workaday world behind as effectively as if you were in the grandest landscape.

A stroll through Elizabeth's back garden presents an entirely different experience that is deeply satisfying to the spirit. Here the transporting effect is almost immediate. Within a few steps, you are immersed in a cool, green space that has the feel and flow of a natural riverbank. Less immediately breathtaking than the dazzling front garden, this area is a study in subdued tints and tones that weave an amazing number of plants into a lacy green web.

Some forty trees, many of them gifts from grandchildren, grace the long beds, which run the full length of the narrow lot. Here Elizabeth used turf grass paths to create the illusion of a smoothly running river. The grassy path pours between the closely planted beds, its green giving way to a brown, bark-covered bridge in a shady spot where grass sulked and moss wore away too quickly. The

The complex plantings celebrate form and texture as well as color. Variegation is used to clarify the shapes of leaf and plant, while butter, cream, and soft, citrusy yellows are splashed about like errant sunshine, bringing light and reflected luster to beds shaded by overhanging trees. Garden of Elizabeth England, Victoria, British Columbia.

slight curves in this main path visually incorporate the trees of distant neighbors into the perimeter plantings. This makes the garden seem even longer than it really is, and encourages the stroller onward to discover what lies beyond the next veil of plants.

At the bottom of the garden, a small thicket of trees blocks the neighbor's house from view. The path now makes an elongated loop, returning behind the main bed so that you see the plants recombined into completely different vignettes and discover entirely new ones. When you arrive back at your starting point, you feel that you have been in another country.

Indeed, like all great gardens, this one is saturated with a sense of both place and person; it is a place to be in its own right, with its own character, and it strongly reflects the character of its maker as well as her deep delight in plants. Combining the very English traits of abundance and enclosure with the Asian sensibility for form and architectural placement, this Canadian stroll garden is further imbued with Elizabeth's own whimsical sense of fun as well as a profound joyfulness. Walking here, one is made constantly aware of the pleasure Elizabeth found in her beloved plants.

An Anglojapanadian Stroll Garden

Some miles away another stroll garden draws more obviously upon the Japanese prototype. Robin Hopper, a transplanted Englishman now living in British Columbia, calls his garden "Anglojapanadian," feeling that three cultures effectively shaped it. Japanese in design, it is full of native Canadian plants (as well as local artwork), and in several areas, beds and borders overflow with English

Three cultures merge in this contemporary stroll garden, where artful objects are placed amid plants that are themselves treated as living artworks. Native woods slide seamlessly into garden plantings that are filled with mixtures of wildflowers and border beauties. Garden of Robin Hopper & Judi Dyelle, Metchosin, British Columbia.

abundance. Hopper and his wife, Judi Dyelle, are both much-awarded potters whose studios and showroom lie at the heart of the garden. Both create unique works from porcelain that are often used as interior decoration or artwork, but both also celebrate the daily in their work by making several full lines of practical pottery as well.

The garden fills the windows of their studios, and their artworks fill the garden, along with sculptural pieces by students and friends. Hopper's work gives him a deep appreciation for the sculptural qualities of plants, and the stroll paths in his garden are made in part to showcase particularly well-shaped native trees and shrubs. The broad paths, barked or graveled, are edged in places with rounded river rocks that create a compelling sense of momentum, leading eye and foot forward. Indeed, the path pours like water, the stony edgings turning it into a wide stream.

In one spot, wedge-shaped mill stones are set into the path, creating a repeating pattern reminiscent of a Japanese family crest. Hopper enjoys playful experimentation, and the garden holds a fascinating variety of paving surfaces, each artfully suited to its setting. Some combine local wood products such as shredded tree bark and wood shavings with rocks dug up on the site. Others involve smooth, rounded river rocks brought from a nearby riverbank, or flat slabs set into concrete.

The long paths lead into and through dark, mature woods, winding through trees that rise like living sculpture amid a flurry of understory shrubs. Several species of native huckleberries *(Vaccinium ovatum, V. parvifolium)* rise in light, airy columns that look amazingly like the delicate, fine-leaved Japanese maples placed nearby. Glossy, broad-leaved salal *(Gaultheria shallon)* scents the spring air with honey from its plump waxen white bells. Holly-like

Oregon grape, both the lower-growing *Mahonia repens* and taller *M. aquifolium*, gleams in shady spots, reflecting light into dim corners with its lacquered leaves.

Along the paths tall sword ferns burst boldly skyward, backed by lacy lady ferns and delicate, drooping maidenhair ferns. Redtwig dogwoods *(Cornus stolonifera)* spread in sheaves of glowing, ruddy stems, while their cousin bunchberry *(Cornus canadensis)* creeps over richly rotting nurse logs on the mossy forest floor. Set among these

Discarded millstone sections spread across the woodland path like fans borrowed from an ancient Japanese family crest. This is a great example of resourceful and artful recycling, adapting local materials for the most functional parts of a garden's design. Garden of Robin Hopper & Judi Dyelle, Metchosin, British Columbia.

An enclosed water garden near the house is strongly Japanesque in flavor, incorporating many design elements from Zen tea gardens, including a small tea hut at the water's edge. The trees and shrubs surrounding the small pool are placed so that their reflections are echoed back to the sky, disturbed now and then by hungry koi seeking their customary snack. Garden of Robin Hopper & Judi Dyelle, Metchosin, British Columbia.

While straight lines are rare both in nature and in naturalistic stroll gardens, this row of western cedars was not planted by human hands. Instead it is the result of natural selection as seedlings jostled for position along a rotting nurse log. The losers died young, while the successful—almost evenly spaced—continue to grow in the moldering compost left by the crumbling mother trunk. Garden of Robin Hopper & Judi Dyelle, Metchosin, British Columbia.

natives are specimen rhododendrons and Japanese maples, each placed in natural niches like living sculpture. In between them are sited artworks in many styles, both serious and playful, forging adventurous links between the natural and the created environment.

Near the house and studios an enclosed garden adapts elements of Zen tea garden design. A small tea house overlooks a series of ponds, where fat koi swim and swooping herons feed. Friends and family often take tea here, admiring the maples and dogwoods surrounding the pond while drinking from cups made for the garden by Judi or Robin. Within the ponds, stepping-stones for water walkers are set atop tall concrete pillars, so the flat stones appear to float on the still pond surface. Small water features are tucked in at every turn, so this enclosed inner garden sings with water music. The flow and fall are varied, so that the water song alters wherever you walk, now a peaceful trickle, now an insistent splashing. Once a stage set designer, Hopper's walls and gates have the dash and flair of good stage sets, and he admits to enjoying "good garden theater."

PLANT PORTRAIT

Lawson Cypress, *Chamaecyparis lawsoniana*

Framework is vital to stroll gardens, where a sense of enclosure is balanced by interior exposure or openings out into areas of overview. Clipped hedges and hard-edged walls are clearly not the best choices when we want to promote an impression of naturalistic layering. Lawson cypress (also called Port Orford cedar) is really a false cypress that reaches 80 feet in the wild. Garden forms are far smaller, and their compact habit and lovely texture make them extremely popular garden plants. They are perhaps best used as a component in tapestry hedging, where small trees and large shrubs are interlayered to produce a ruffled, unclipped green wall. Naturally, golden, purple, and blue-grey foliage plants can be added in where stronger colorist effects are wanted.

In stroll gardens, where greenery is a keynote, the subtle colors of various Lawson cypress forms blend unobtrusively with other trees and shrubs, coming into their own in winter, when their plumed and drooping branches glitter brilliantly. Lawson cypress has a naturally conical shape, and its smallest form, 'Ellwoodii' (to 9'), is an ideal framework plant for urban gardens. The somewhat taller 'Wisselii' (to 18') has a looser, more eccentric shape, which makes it well suited to a stroll garden setting, where character is prized. Golden forms such as 'Lutea' and 'Golden King' (to 30') need room to develop their full potential.

PLANT PORTRAIT

Star Magnolia, *Magnolia stellata*

Small trees with individual charm make excellent center-pieces for stroll gardens. Star magnolia is hardy to Zone 4, and many forms are small enough to suit tiny urban gardens. Although this Japanese species sheds its glossy leaves in fall, the silky young stems are invitingly strokable in winter, when the open architecture of the plant is revealed. Star magnolia looks great naked, and spring brings even greater glory when this shrubby little tree is smothered beneath its masses of ribbon-petaled blossoms, pink, white, or rosy, which often persist into summer. The large leaves give it an exotic appearance that accords well with hardy tropicals, yet it also blends unobtrusively among native plantings. Multitrunked specimens develop great character in maturity, making them ideal stroll garden denizens.

Round-headed and arching, the curving canopy of star magnolia is pleasingly irregular, as are its twisting, multiple trunks. Slow growing, this small tree is an excellent choice where space is limited. It grows well in urban settings, where buildings offer protection from early frosts that can nip its tender buds in late winter. Sunrise Gardens, designed by Bobbie Garthwaite & Joe Sullivan, Bainbridge Island, Washington.

American Mixed
Borders

American Mixed Borders

chapter 5

Mixed borders hold plants of every kind, scaled to suit the available space but always planted to reflect the four tiers found in nature: trees, shrubs, perennials, and ground covers. With their high proportion of woody

plants, well-planted mixed borders are relatively independent and easy to care for, remaining sturdily attractive between grooming sessions. The original models were

Richly interwoven, spilling over with plants of every kind and size, this layered mixed border is unified by its tightly integrated design, which plays artfully off the shapes, textures, and colors of each plant. Every plant is placed both for contrast and for echoes, which creates comforting repeats of every attribute—shape, size, form, texture, and color. Garden of Valerie Murray, Victoria, British Columbia.

created for English estate gardens, where they were intended to shine from late spring into fall. American mixed borders differ chiefly in being year-round plantings that never go off duty.

Because American yards and gardens are small, many American gardeners work hard to create structural plantings that hold their looks in every season. Because most American gardeners manage their plots alone or without trained help, American mixed borders are by necessity less demanding than the English prototypes, whose upkeep can be as rigorous as that of herbaceous perennial borders. If American mixed borders are essentially practical plantings,

Inner topography can be created by playing with plants, moving them about while still in their pots until a satisfying series of contrasts and repeats develops. Time is a player here, since so many plants change size dramatically over the course of a few seasons. Editing helps preserve the balance of forms, as will the use of annuals and short-lived plants as fillers during the first years of a border's life. Garden of Ernie & Marietta O'Byrne, Eugene, Oregon.

their simplified basis does not mean that summer beauty must be sacrificed. When their principle plant elements are chosen with care, these efficient mixed borders can deliver as much color and seasonal flow of change as their prima donna forerunners.

Mixed borders have been slowly gaining followers across the United States, beginning in the warmer regions where the English models could be more closely approximated. North and South Carolina are mixed border hot spots, and the trend continues across the belt line of America, roughly following the pattern of the USDA hardiness Zone 8. Across the continent, the maritime Northwest has given rise to some of the most unusual and creatively interpreted mixed borders to date. From the internationally acclaimed Bellevue Botanical Garden borders near Seattle to the tiny mixed borders that fill urban lots from Victoria to San Francisco, these Northwestern gardens are noteworthy for their attempts—very often successful—to stretch the garden year. Gentle climate, lovely native flora, and eagerly experimental gardeners all help to further this noble cause. Until recently, many Northwesterners restricted themselves to genre gardening, creating collections of rhododendrons and azaleas, heaths and heathers, roses or perennials. The American mixed border provides an excellent framework for artfully combining woody plants with perennials, bulbs, and ground covers.

Given the high percentage of woody plants in the American mixed borders, it is not surprising that naturalistic layering is intrinsic to this developing design school, whose garden models are readily adaptable to any space and style. Nearly always, their overlapping, interwoven plantings have the soft-edged look of mixed deciduous and coniferous woods. Because they echo those natural planting patterns, these borders display a more intriguing inner topography than do most formally designed borders. Their pleasingly eccentric, nonsymmetrical plantings create an interior rise and fall of shape, an ebb and flow of form and habit that results in dramatically changing views, depending on the angle from which the borders are examined. In such gardens, there is always more to be discovered, since each fresh viewpoint discloses previously unseen plants and juxtapositions. This is particularly true when a variety of plant sizes and shapes are alternated and woven throughout the borders.

The same design principles that direct the composition of paintings inform naturalistic mixed borders, in which plant shape is paramount. Larger-scaled planting patterns (or extended vignettes) are developed by selecting and repeating plants with a specific form. Many shape-inspired planters like to work with a basic triangle pattern, in which a relatively large and spire-tipped plant provides the tapering height, and flanking plants create a wider, spreading base. Mixed dwarf and compact conifers lend themselves readily to such patterns, and combining them with heathers and heaths, grasses and densely twiggy shrubs produces marvelous living tapestries with extended seasonal color. Perennials and bulbs are tucked into pockets within these woody frames, adding more seasonal flow and change than woody ghetto gardens (like those unrelieved rhododendron collections) can afford. This basic visual and physical pattern is extremely adaptable, and although the results look very different if applied to a shady, wetland planting or a sunny, open one, the subtle similarities are discovered by the eye, if not the brain, and make for a satisfying impression of continuity between various parts of the garden.

In closely planted borders it's important to leave enough room for the full shape of each plant to be appreciated. Here plants are interwoven so that they overlap in a friendly, casual manner without crowding. Each plant's similarities and differences are apparent, making for high visual interest. Imagine a same-sized plot planted only with pachysandra. Garden of Ernie & Marietta O'Byrne, Eugene, Oregon.

One of the most enjoyable projects for an advancing garden maker is to rework existing summery borders (mixed or not) after this naturalistic pattern. The addition of appropriate evergreen and multiseasonal plants will quickly extend the flow of color from earliest spring through autumn. An invigorating infusion of structural plants throughout the beds as well as around them will provide enclosure, support perennial displays, and make attractive evergreen island groupings that hold up as integrated shapes even under snow cover.

Western Naturalistic Mixed Borders

Western gardens are increasingly influenced by our developing sense of place. As regional schools and novel gardening styles emerge, our gardens are fast becoming less imitative and more directly reflective of the realities of our particular environment. Where older gardens were highly control-based, contemporary gardens tend to depend on cooperation between people and plants. As we become less drawn to living out or expressing dominance in our relationship with the natural, we can begin instead to explore the new ground opened up by our growing ecological sensibilities. The most exciting new design trends involve planting in like-minded communities, using plants architecturally, and placing them so that their inherent and specific strengths are assets.

Naturalistic border communities are primarily based on shared cultural requirements. Plants that demand excellent drainage are made happy on sloping, gravely sites. Plants that enjoy damp shade are accommodated by placement in a naturally boggy area. Though this sounds entirely sensible (and so it is), the concept is nonetheless mildly revolutionary. A few years ago most of us would have tried (urged on by professional advice) to drain that boggy ground rather than to plant it appropriately. The poor, gravely site would have been richly improved, the high ground leveled, and the low ground elevated. Uniformity was considered a worthy goal. Our gardens were not expected to reflect where we lived so much as what an ideal garden ought to be. These are large assumptions to be left unexplored, and yet they were for generations. The fact that what is ideal in England or Ireland or Scotland or France is probably unworkable in Minnesota or Florida or Arizona was immaterial. No matter where we lived, many of us strove to recreate gardens of other times and places. Only over the past few decades, with the dawning of an expanded ecological and regional awareness, have we begun to consider garden plantings in terms of creating habitat or discovering existing ecological niches.

These days many of us hope that the land and plants we tend will be actively improved under our stewardship. Often this begins with a desire to garden without resorting to poisonous chemical interventions. Simply by not using

---

Naturalistic garden designers often play with traditional forms and patterns, altering them to reflect the realities of time and place. Here, an allée of standard 'PeeGee' hydrangeas ends in a cluster of conifers that echo the evergreen woods beyond. Though repetition gives it coherence, a charming irregularity of line and planting prevents this area of a large, naturalistic garden from looking unsuitably formal. Madrona garden, designed by Michael Schultz & Geoff Beasley, Sherwood, Oregon.

toxic chemical fixes for everything from weeds to plant diseases, we can benefit soil, water, and air quality in and beyond our immediate neighborhood. The next step, for many gardeners, is to alter their approach to garden planting. Rather than growing whatever plants we happen upon at the nearest garden center, we start seeking out plants that are appropriate to the actual setting we can offer them. In order to do this well, we begin learning as much as we can about where we are and what micro-climates we have available. All of these concerns are

Naturalistic mixed borders reflect site, setting, and the taste of the garden maker, as well as regional realities. They may draw upon many design traditions, adapting the most suitable concepts and reshaping them to carry out the designer's intentions. These layered plantings make visual ladders that integrate a bevy of border beauties with towering native trees. The winding paths are wide enough for company, yet make the small space seem extensive. Garden of Elizabeth Lair, Eugene, Oregon.

addressed when we begin experimenting with naturalistic mixed borders in which every niche is developed and planted with the plants' satisfaction as much in mind as our own.

Designing Naturalistic Mixed Borders

As mentioned, the classic English mixed borders are summer creatures, but in America, the trend is to develop mixed borders that extend the garden year as much as possible. Because our gardens are generally modest in size

Building borders around existing native trees like these garry oaks gives gardens instant presence and a strong sense of place. It also encourages us to pay attention to their sculptural strength, matching it with appropriate proportions of space and planting. Companion beds must be substantial enough in mass and strong enough in form to read against that natural grandeur without imposing on the aging trees' root systems. Garden of Valerie Murray, Victoria, British Columbia.

Unless components are selected with great care, borders that hold a high percentage of conifers can look stiff and artificial. When a full range of shape, size, and texture is employed, our borders can achieve a lovely flow of form. Infusions of broad-leaved evergreens, deciduous shrubs, and soft-textured grasses give this naturalistic mixed border great character in every season. Garden of Ernie & Marietta O'Byrne, Eugene, Oregon.

and scope and because we don't usually have a staff to carry out our orders (wouldn't that be lovely!), our gardens need to serve us rather differently than those sumptuous estate garden models. In huge gardens there is room for every season to have its own space, with spring borders, fall color borders, even winter gardens; if the summery herbaceous or mixed border is barren for six months of the year, other areas will compensate. Where one small space is all we have to work with, we tend to want the parts we see every day to look attractive all year.

American mixed borders are designed to be comfortable and mutually supportive communities, where many plants share ground space cooperatively. As a rule of thumb, a good percentage of the woody perimeter and backbone plants involved will be evergreen. Depending on climate, perhaps a quarter to a third of these will be conifers. An excess of conifers gives a mixed border a stiff, rather formal look, but in colder climates, where most broad-leaved evergreens are tender, it is difficult to create adequate enclosure without relying heavily on these sturdy candidates. So while climate will determine the mixture you can use, no matter where you live adding

Naturalistic layering can be achieved in a very small space. In narrow borders slim, upright plants with a variety of habits and textures create a pleasingly ruffled effect, even though the entire bed is just a few feet deep. Vines trained to cover the wall disguise its hard edge and make a rippling backdrop for the shining golden Japanese maple and stiff-fingered golden honeysuckle, *Lonicera nitida* 'Baggesen's Gold'. Garden of Elizabeth England, Victoria, British Columbia.

In the sunny front garden at Madrona, sweeps of mixed conifers are softened with masses of perennials and self-sown annuals. In every season the strong lines of the evergreens boldly echo the mixed conifers and deciduous trees of the native woods that surround the garden. Madrona garden, designed by Michael Schultz & Geoff Beasley, Sherwood, Oregon.

structural woody plants in these proportional quantities will lend a summery, perennial-based border greater architectural strength and a longer season of vitality almost immediately.

The layers found in natural plant communities suggest the patterns in which mixed border plantings are arranged: Trees large and small shelter a range of ornamental shrubs that are in turn underskirted with perennials, bulbs, and ground covers. Vines lace back and forth between the whole, weaving them into a tightly knit community. Artfully and irregularly arrayed, these tiers of plants act as visual ladders to carry the eye up to the largest elements in both the garden and the overall environment, matching them in scale. Transitional plantings also bring the eye back down to the more intimate scale of the garden, linking the big picture firmly to the smaller, more detailed scene within the garden beds and borders.

The best place to see all these ideas at work is in one of the most exciting mixed border gardens in the country. The result of a stimulating partnership between a talented and risk-taking designer, Michael Schultz, and garden owners Geoff Beasley and Jim Sampson, this ever-expanding garden grew from simple beginnings into a green explosion that turned Geoff into a visionary garden maker in his own right while still including active participation and support from the other two partners in this ambitious enterprise. Tucked into the rolling hills outside Portland, Oregon, the 5-acre garden encompasses native woods, meadows, swamp, and a dry hillside. Named "Madrona," after the presiding native trees *(Arbutus menziesii)*, this multifaceted mixed border garden combines native habitat and imaginative, extravagant plantings in an extraordinarily generous and captivating manner.

At Madrona, the house is encircled by gardens, each of which embodies a different mood. The sunny front yard is overlooked by a deep, shadowy porch that becomes a bower of vines in summer. The shady side yard is a meditative retreat, its small porch a quiet place to listen to the rain. Madrona garden, designed by Michael Schultz & Geoff Beasley, Sherwood, Oregon.

Near the house shady pockets alternate with sunny patches, and the surrounding garden displays strikingly different moods to explore. One porch sits in deep shade, overlooking an ebullient dry river that flows with flowers and foliage. A sunnier one rises in an overlook above a long, semiformal walk, while a third makes a minute refuge, hushed and still and saturated in green. Everywhere, enormous native trees are treated like architectural treasures; the paths wind around them, and large beds surround their massive trunks. Many of these beds are small shrines to the garden makers' fallen companions, places where scattered ashes keep friends ever-present to memory.

In the sunny upper garden, a wide, stony border blends woody plants in profusion, mixed with softening sweeps of bulbs and perennials. Designed as a woody winter border, this young planting will also serve to screen the garden from future development as neighboring properties fall to the bulldozer. At the far end from the house, this border ends in a ruffle of madronas under which large, twiggy compost heaps have become home to

myriad birds, snakes, and other small creatures. These brush piles are too much in service to disturb, so other compost areas have been established that can be mined for the garden without disturbing nests or hiding places. Here the garden curves down in steps, opening into a white moon garden, filled with pale plants that reflect light in the evening and by night. Nearby is a large barn that houses a guest suite for Michael Schultz, who remains closely connected with this ongoing garden project.

Beneath the barn the land tumbles downhill through dark woods, emerging at a boggy area that contains a small pond in summer and a good-sized swamp in all seasons. Here gardening is largely restorative, as existing native plantings have been preserved and encouraged to spread. Persistent Northwestern weeds such as ivy, nettles, and the Himalayan blackberry (imported by Luther Burbank to add vigor to the mild-mannered local strain) are ruthlessly removed. Several seating areas have been developed, including private meditation nooks and a small amphitheater that has seen everything from musical and theatrical performances to memorial services. Along the bridged path linking the damp lower garden and the house, giant gunneras have been brought in for the sheer magic of their elephant-sized leaves. Elsewhere, imported plantings are few, although beyond the wooded slope, a sunny, dry hillside exposed years ago by logging is being planted with natives of Oregon and California. Here the brilliantly colored wild grape *Vitis californica* 'Roger's Red' scrambles through low manzanitas and shrubby ceanothus. The new web of shrubs and small trees has already begun to link the meadow and the woods, and to recreate the ragged-edged layers lost to clearing that occurred before the land was purchased.

The natural bog and swampy areas have been left largely undisturbed and are always alive with birds. Where the path leads down from the house and near several seating areas, combined plantings of natives and exotics make a gentle transition from the wild to the garden. Madrona garden, designed by Michael Schultz & Geoff Beasley, Sherwood, Oregon.

Where clipped hedges once framed these borders, a looser look now prevails. Tall, spiky plants direct the eye upward and echo the jutting thrust of the backdrop trees. Madrona garden, designed by Michael Schultz & Geoff Beasley, Sherwood, Oregon.

PLANT PORTRAIT

Madrona, *Arbutus menziesii*

No tree in the woods is more beautiful or more exotic-looking than the red-barked madrona, whose sinuous lines provide such telling contrast to arrow-straight Douglas firs and shaggy hemlocks. Though wildlings are notoriously difficult to transplant, seed-grown madronas take to garden life with ease, growing quickly into statuesque plants of tremendous character and distinction. Their survival is most threatened by excess summer water, so it is vital to place sprinklers or automatic water systems well away from the present and future root zone of these majestic trees. These evergreens shed their dead leaves and splat red berries over a wide area, so it is also wise not to position seating areas or patios where madrona litter will be an annoyance. In shady settings madronas make excellent canopy trees above plantings of azaleas, rhododendrons, and small maples. In sunnier spots, underskirt them with California lilacs *(Ceanothus* species) and glossy Oregon grape *(Mahonia aquifolium)*.

The ruddy, peeling bark and majestically arching trunks of madronas *(Arbutus menziesii)* give the lucky gardens they inhabit a look of power and grace. Intolerant of summer irrigation and frequent root disturbance, these regal trees make an excellent backdrop for a painterly bed, but are themselves best underplanted with natives that enjoy similar conditions (like salal and huckleberries). Madrona garden, designed by Michael Schultz & Geoff Beasley, Sherwood, Oregon.

PLANT PORTRAIT

Strawberry Tree, *Arbutus unedo*

In smaller gardens the more compact strawberry tree (Zone 7, 12'–30') will fit more readily. Generally a large shrub, this neat-leaved evergreen achieves small treehood over time and in favored settings. Charmingly sinuous trunks give these dapper shrubs pronounced character even at a young age, particularly when multitrunked specimens are set amid creeping bunchberry *(Cornus canadensis)* and evergreen, winter-blooming sweet box *(Sarcococca humilis)*. Like their cousins, strawberry trees offer rusty, peeling bark and drooping clusters of waxy, pale pink-and-cream flowers that are even handsomer than those of the big madronas. The fruits of the strawberry tree are plump and pimpled, looking like a tasty treat. They are indeed edible, but the Latin name, *unedo*, means "I eat one," and the implication is well taken. In any case, the attractive fruits are best left on the shrub, where they bob like delightful little lanterns in the winter winds.

As the garden moves away from the house, it grows progressively wilder. A shifting mixture of native and garden plants are interwoven in natural-looking borders that merge almost imperceptibly into the wild. Madrona garden, designed by Michael Schultz & Geoff Beasley, Sherwood, Oregon.

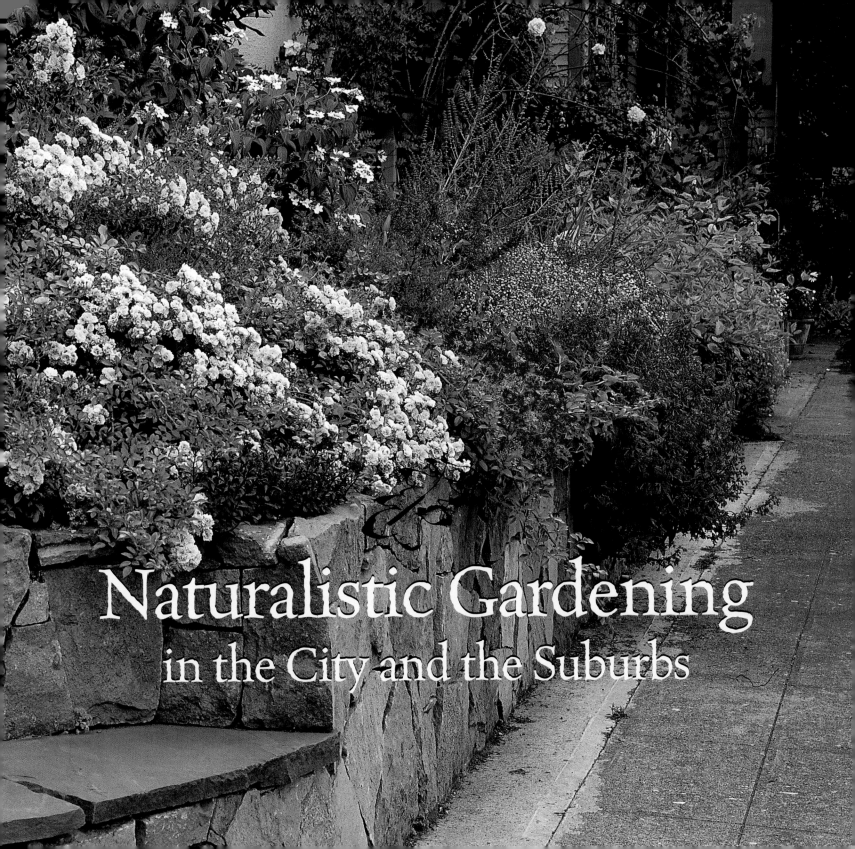

Naturalistic Gardening
in the City and the Suburbs

Naturalistic Gardening
in the City and the Suburbs

chapter 6

My favorite city gardens shelter the garden maker in a leafy green nest while also inviting participation from passersby. Sidewalk gardens may offer attractive benches where neighbors and strangers can rest. Tiny

front yards may spill over with scented plants that send their perfume out to the streets, refreshing the spirits of all who come along. One Portland garden involves a whole

---

Layered, naturalistic planting transforms this tiny, narrow urban lot into an ever-changing bower of fragrance and color. No passerby fails to stop and smell the roses, admire the lilies, or exchange compliments with the enchanting gardener, now in her eighties, whose loving hands keep the garden in good trim. Garden of Connie Caunt, Victoria, British Columbia.

neighborhood, where parking strips and front yards bubble over with blossoms. Street-side hammocks and seats are heaped with cozy blankets and pillows; sidewalk kiosks are stocked with books and an illustrated, house-by-house historical overview of the area; and a thermos of hot tea is always available for strollers to savor. In Seattle, a miniature sidewalk garden has a hand-painted sign encouraging people to pick flowers to take home. Amazingly, the garden was ablaze with bloom, and if people were indeed taking up the kindly offer, the garden was in no way diminished by the generosity of its owner. (This would never have worked in my old neighborhood, where

roving guru followers routinely stripped the front beds, screaming uncharitable remarks about running dog capitalists when anyone protested. Indeed, *my* sign said, "Please leave the flowers for all of us to enjoy." Oh well.)

In the city, gardening of any kind is a gift to everybody, providing a welcome respite from asphalt and concrete. Naturalistic gardens, with their abundant layering and luxuriant plants, provide an especially compelling antidote to straight lines and hard edges. When the relentless geometry of urban buildings and roads starts to look normal, wandering stems and untrammeled flurries of green leaves provide vital relief for human senses, reminding us that the value of order is relative. Over time, deprived of the direct experience of natural settings, we can

A few steps off the city sidewalk, this enticing gate creates a miniature vista that clever paving has made appear almost limitless. When the gate is opened, the gently curving path calls the eye toward the garden's end, which is veiled in mystery. Although the actual space involved is extremely small, and large apartments loom on either side, adept planting screens the garden completely from within, its irregularly stacked tiers successfully disguising the lines and angles of nearby walls. Garden designed by Eryl Morton, Victoria, British Columbia.

lose our sense of place in the world. Perhaps this loss is at the root of that dominance-based design school that dictates periodic military brush-cuts for every plant, regardless of its kind or size, and advocates vacuuming the soil until it is truly *clean*. Dirty dirt? Horrors! Not in my garden! When order is divorced from nature and allowed to rule our lives and that of our plants, tidiness and control can come to seem more important than natural beauty.

Since scrupulously tidy urban gardens are quite common, it is fascinating to watch the reactions of passersby when they come across a garden in which plants are permitted to express the full flow of their unfettered spirits. Over the years, I have taken notes on this in a number of urban garden settings, including my old home in Seattle's Capitol Hill area. No matter where the garden is located, the first response of the passersby is the same: a smile, followed quickly by a deep sigh. Shoulders drop as neck tension drains away. In less than a minute most people demonstrate a markedly more relaxed posture. Though I took care to remain out of sight whenever possible during my observation stints, not once did I ever see anybody show signs of disapproval or scorn about the garden's lack of obvious control. Indeed, I never once overheard a negative comment of any kind. Almost everybody reacted in some way, and the response was overwhelmingly positive, even joyful. That has intrigued me for years: Can it be that precision gardeners simply don't look at other people's gardens? Or is it possible that they, too, admire the luxuriant abundance in other people's naturalistic gardens?

I will probably never know, but I do know that transforming a sterile city lot into a verdant garden rewards both the gardener and every person who is exposed to that garden. I experienced the truth of this daily in my tiny Seattle garden, where total strangers stopped on the way home from work to help me weed and left presents of manure and lily bulbs, rose food, and plump dahlia tubers on the front porch. Often these gifts were accompanied by little notes saying, "For the garden," or "Thanks for sharing." Sometimes they came with advice and commentary. ("When are you going to thin that lilac?" and "I liked the striped blue iris you grew last year better than that fat purple one you have now.") Sometimes plants were simply dropped off with no word to indicate why. That was all right because I didn't really need words; I have seen many times how gardens can make friends out of strangers.

Gardens That Reach Out

One of my favorite gardens is what I call a garden advance, rather than a retreat. These gardens have the knack for making friends in seconds. In an older section of Portland, Oregon, Lucy and Fred Hardiman have created a garden that functions as a coffeehouse or outdoor café for the entire neighborhood. The area holds an interesting blend of modest homes and family businesses, its small streets full of smaller shops. Mom-and-pop groceries, aging-hippie boutiques, Latino bodegas, and a Buddhist temple are visited by steady streams of people who are themselves varied and diverse, of all kinds, all colors, all shapes and sizes. The Hardiman garden encircles a pair of Victorian homes, beautifully restored by Fred. Both buildings are always full of people: the Hardiman's daughter and her friends, neighbors and renters from next door. Nearly all of the renters are artists, most of whom contribute art of one kind or another to

the shared gardens. The same communal, cooperative spirit that inspires shared housing, shared gardens, and shared ideals overflows both house and garden and spills out into the street.

A few years ago, when the retaining wall of the front garden needed replacement, Lucy decided she wanted to incorporate a large bench into the new wall. Now the front garden embraces the sidewalk and street, rather than walling it out. The wall-top plantings tumble into the street, pouring out fragrance and color that can be seen for blocks. The sidewalk surrounding the garden is always full of strolling neighbors. In the morning they arrive to chat, coffee cups in hand (these are replaced by wine glasses in the evening). At any time of day somebody is sitting out there, sipping tea or reading the newspaper. Women with babies in strollers, old men enjoying a revolting cigar that blurs the scent of roses and honeysuckle, or lanky young kids, skateboards at their feet, hair bristling blue in towering mohawks, all stop to rest and take in the amazing floral display.

When Lucy and Fred made the new wall and resting area, it was with precisely this kind of neighborhood interaction in mind. "People in the city need to be in gardens,"

The handsome stone wall turns the front garden into a gigantic container planting for a gardener who revels in creating luxuriantly naturalistic mixed plantings in every possible medium. Geraniums, poppies, salvias, and a tumble of herbs strive to outbloom each other all summer long, while the striped paddles of *Canna* x 'Pretoria' continue to stretch themselves skyward. Garden of Lucy & Fred Hardiman, Portland, Oregon.

says Lucy firmly. "We wanted to make sure that everybody could enjoy the garden as much as we do."

Now hundreds of people a day admire the Hardimans' ever-changing garden as it cycles through the seasons. In winter, the bloodtwig dogwood, *Cornus alba* 'Gouchaltii', drops its pink-and-gold-splashed leaves, revealing the vigorously upright habit hidden by the large and glorious foliage. Nearby, ruffled spikes of statuesque *Euphorbia* x 'Jade Dragon' remain triumphantly shapely in all weathers. Blooming in February and March, this marvelous spurge holds its enormous, balloonlike clusters of bracts until fall. In earliest spring the scents of a dozen shrubs and vines tantalize the nose; one February day mine discovered wafts of spice and honey coming from honeysuckle (*Lonicera standishii*), *Viburnum* x *bodnantense* 'Dawn', and winter hazel (*Hamamelis mollis* 'Pallida', which is the most fragrant form), all mingling with a succession of perfumed daphnes. In summer huge balls of *Allium schubertii* explode like spangled starbursts, the seedheads holding their magnificent form for months on end. Huge, striped paddle-like leaves of *Canna* 'Pretoria' leap up above sprawls of wild honeywort, *Cerinthe major* 'Purpurea'. Summer also brings an endless parade of roses, which wind through fences, clamber over the arched entry gate, and climb up arbors and trellises. All of them are fragrant, many intensely so, and their combined scent—the living breath of the garden—permeates the entire neighborhood on warm summery nights. In autumn there are still dozens of blossoms on the climbers dangling from a cherry tree in the side yard. Much visited by neighborhood children, this tree is often broken by their efforts to eat the fat fruits. In his typical manner, Fred is working on a way to make the cherries more accessible without harming the tree or the roses.

The backyard is enclosed in layer upon layer of plantings, as trees give way to lower shrubs and drifting masses of perennials. Screened from the street, the back garden is a retreat for family and friends, including the lucky tenants of the adjacent house, who often share meals and music in the lingering twilight of summer evenings. Next door to the paired houses, a vegetable garden liberally laced with flowers is shared by all three households, each taking on a share of work and all enjoying the results of their collective labors. Doubling the backyard gave Lucy more scope than is common in city lots, where space is generally at a premium. She has the luxury of being able to plant large perimeter trees, like magnolias and cherries, using small, delicate trees like stewartias and Japanese maples in the garden's interior. Lapping layers of shrubs hide the tree's knees and build up effective screening between neighboring properties. Indeed, in summer, it is easy to feel lost in a wilderness of blossom here, especially when you stumble upon the snug hidden seats that are tucked here and there throughout the garden.

Lucy's favorite summer lounging spot is a wide bench heaped with soft cushions to make a delicious couch. Snuggled just beneath a fence that is itself hidden beneath a tangle of greenery, the couch can hardly be seen in high season, making it an ideal spot for garden snoozing. My particular favorite spot is perfect for people watching without being seen. Set just within the entry gate, the small bench is half buried under pots of newly acquired plants (a large and constantly changing category). Almost hidden from view, the bench is so full of flowerpots that it hardly has room for visitors, but those who squeeze themselves in find rewards for both eye and nose. That, after all, is the keynote of such a garden. Full of lovely flowers and fragrant surprises, it is a cornucopia of generosity, a boon for the street and all who travel there, extending to each a haunting, delightful taste of wild nature in the heart of the city.

Public Gardening in a Private Home

Further north, in the charming, quirky old James Bay neighborhood of Victoria, British Columbia, a truly tiny garden manages to achieve an astonishing degree of presence, sharing its wild bounty with aplomb. Over many years, an extraordinary plantswoman, now in her eighties, has created a community of extremely well grown plants that interlace and interlayer cooperatively, each taking center stage in turns throughout the year. A specialist in a dozen kinds of flowers, from florist's auriculas to old roses and species clematis, Connie Caunt has turned her small garden into a horticulturist's dream. Sweetly scented shrubs spill over the low fence, inviting attention with constantly changing displays of color and living perfume. Rambling, scrambling roses thread through a gnarled cherry tree near the front door. In spring, heavy with bloom, the cherry pours its scent down the street to mix with the fresh salt breeze from nearby James Bay.

Public benches extend the garden's reach, making it accessible to hundreds of people each day. Hidden ones are retreats that benefit the gardener, offering privacy and a stimulating sense of being enclosed within the garden. Looming plants rise overhead, softer forms foam at your feet, and you are enfolded in the garden's soft green heart. Garden of Lucy & Fred Hardiman, Portland, Oregon.

Tiny, tidy, and charmingly naturalistic, the garden is threaded with narrow paths just big enough for one small person. Despite the remarkably limited space, Connie prefers winding paths that make their casual way between house and tree, shrub and shed. On either side of the backyard, enclosing fences are swathed in clematis and roses, often paired for overlapping seasons of blossom. The well-filled beds hold a wide array of plants, which are allowed to create their own communities. Connie provides editing and nurturing, but she finds the serendipity of a brilliantly placed, self-sown seedling to be as satisfying as anything she thought up herself. "I let the plants put themselves where they want to be, then I decide how long they can stay there," she explains with a chuckle. As a result, the house walls, front steps, and the retaining wall that frames the small rock garden are all studded with seedlings, for like me, Connie likes to see plants taking over territory, blooming in cracks and crannies where we would never dream of trying to make them grow.

The front yard is fully visible from the street, and Connie takes care to provide as many lovely things for

Open or shut, a garden gate offers an implicit welcome to street strollers, who can gaze past the low barrier and feast their senses for free on the extravaganza of bloom within the garden. In this tiny urban oasis, roses form looping arches, lace into trees, and tumble carelessly into the street, offering themselves to all takers. Garden of Connie Caunt, Victoria, British Columbia.

In very small gardens, there is only room for one tree. The cherry tree that overhangs the front door dominates this little urban garden, boasting spring flowers, summer fruit, fall foliage color, and a potent winter silhouette. The little beds hold an astonishing succession of flowers, for winter and spring bulbs are sandwiched among summer and autumn perennials. All are chosen for adaptability and cooperative spirit, so they thrive without a great deal of fussing. Garden of Connie Caunt, Victoria, British Columbia.

people to enjoy as she can. In back, however, the enclosed space is a snug little hideaway for Connie and her beloved cats, who lounge languidly in the sunniest spots. They quite obviously find places where they can keep an eye on Connie and make sure she doesn't pay so much attention to the garden that there is no time for them, for a cat's sense of proportion is infallible. Besides cat sunbathing spots, the little yard holds a few warm, sheltered beds where Connie grows special strawberries in cold frames to discourage voracious slugs, and just enough sweet corn to give herself a treat several times a week in high summer. Here and there stand special shrubs such as a native red currant *(Ribes sanguineum)* draped with small clematis, and elderly fruit trees holding up long-limbed roses.

In this naturalistic urban garden, species clematis cling to walls, interlace through shrubs, and clamber into trees. Here one runs across the front of a narrow border, spangling its ruffled leaves with a froth of scented, starry flowers. Garden of Connie Caunt, Victoria, British Columbia.

The narrow paths are mulched with trimmings and twigs gleaned from the cherry tree, whose fruit stems are also used in the special potting mixtures Connie blends for persnickety plants. Garden of Connie Caunt, Victoria, British Columbia.

In this garden nothing is wasted, all is recycled, and every spent flower or fallen leaf ends up as compost or mulch. The open-sided potting shed is packed with dozens of boxes and tins and sacks and tubs, each holding a single ingredient. Dried cherry leaves in one, the wiry fruit stems in another, here moldering oak leaves, there shredded bracken ferns or a box of tiny twigs, neatly clipped. Other ingredients are involved as well, including charcoal to sweeten acid soil, bone meal for nourishment, greensand and granite dust, even clean cat litter to add clay granules to plants that prefer retentive soils. Like a fine chef, Connie concocts special mixtures for each kind of plant, from florists' primroses to sweet corn. Her beloved roses and clematis are heavy feeders that require supplemental feeding (often with aged manure and alfalfa pellets) several times a season to keep them productive. Collections of species and specialists' show primroses are ranged in tidy rows along the top of the cat enclosure, just out of reach of stretching paws. Below them, neat little shelves hold assortments of fine-textured sedums and succulents that Connie rearranges constantly, making tiny wild gardens in pans and trays for friends, and creating enchanting small worlds of intertwined plants in which you can lose yourself utterly.

Her rock garden, too, is appropriately miniature and planted in the same naturalistic manner that characterizes the rest of the garden. Although the rock garden is built upon orderly rows of hollow bricks, the planting patterns are casual and loose. At every turn, plants are spilling over and dripping down the sides, arranging themselves in pleasing partnerships and tiny bouquets. "I really like the hollow bricks as planters, because they make it so easy to replace a failing plant with a fresh one without disturbing the roots of anything else," Connie notes. "They are also light enough for me to move by myself, so I can rearrange things whenever I like."

She feels that such independence is part of the secret of long-term successful gardening. "I always try to do as much as possible by myself, and part of what makes things

A row of hollow bricks displays charming combinations of small herbs, choice rock plants, and florists' flowers. Mossy colonies soften sharp edges, and self-sown seedlings are often left to bloom undisturbed. Garden of Connie Caunt, Victoria, British Columbia.

possible is choosing plants that don't need very much attention in the first place," she says. All around her, interlayered plants prove her point, making memorable pictures more potent than mere words.

Suburban Mixed Borders

In rural settings where natural habit is relatively intact, there are a great many visual cues to guide the garden

maker. There the challenge is to make convincing transitions between real habitat and the artfully arranged garden plants. The task is somewhat different in suburban situations, particularly where the integrity of such native communities as still exist has long ago been compromised. Even in wooded areas, neighboring houses may be so close as to make functional screening both necessary and difficult. In newer suburbs, there may be almost nothing to work with in the early years of a garden. This can be freeing as well as frustrating, for without existing native plantings to set the tone, we can create a neo-native community, placing every element precisely where we choose.

In my own backyard, as at the Madrona garden, very young mixed naturalistic borders are reweaving the ancient web that once linked the tall woodland trees to a damp meadow at the bottom of a slope. When we first saw the cottage we now rent (on a small island near Seattle), the site soil had been scraped to hardpan, and no vegetative traces remained to tell us what kind of soil we had to work with. Our first step was to bring in 80 yards of sandy loam which we used to reshape the barren and awkwardly tilted hillside, restoring the original, less abrupt grade changes that we deduced from several small strips of standing trees

Berming the soil brought it back up to the original grade and preserved the health of the largest trees that separate two closely spaced houses. Both owners benefit from the screening created by the mixed plantings that supplement the natives. The blending of small trees, shrubs, perennials, and ground covers reproduces the layers of the woodland in the background. Lovejoy/Rogers garden, Bainbridge Island, Washington.

Within the mixed borders the same layering patterns are displayed in miniature. The plants are arranged for high contrast of form and texture, which gives them a lively quality of movement and flow. This bed is shown about a year after planting. Lovejoy/Rogers garden, Bainbridge Island, Washington.

left by the developers. Many of these had exposed roots that were left hanging several feet above the new soil level. We filled in around them, making gently sloping berms and beds between neighboring houses and the brand-new cottage as space allowed.

These beds and berms were quickly planted with fast-growing natives, mainly willows and shrubby dogwoods, to provide screening and privacy. Small trees and ornamental shrubs were woven between the taller plantings, creating a tapestry hedge that blocked views and muffled sound, yet let in air and light. Behind the cottage a narrow wedge of original woods made a partial barrier between our garden and a very large new house next door. Here our intention was to repair as best we might the transitional areas between the deep woods and the raw garden site, which was described by the city planner as resembling the surface of the moon. To make better planting areas immediately, we layered raised beds with sandy loam and composted dairy manure, creating a lean but tilthy soil mix that drains well. The great majority of both native and garden plants do well in such soils, so long as greedy feeders like tea roses are avoided.

Though the garden is still very young (the pictures were taken between twelve and eighteen months after initial planting), the plantings are already beginning to integrate

The cottage is encircled by overlapping layers of plants that emulate the richly interwoven woodlands behind it. A small graveled seating area doubles as a Tai Chi practice area and divides the garden from the long meadow that falls away toward the stream. Lovejoy/Rogers garden, Bainbridge Island, Washington.

Changes of grade can be hard to handle in small gardens. Here the steep side yard was terraced into two beds divided by a gravel path, which was stepped down irregularly rather than geometrically in order to follow the line of the hillside. Lovejoy/Rogers garden, Bainbridge Island, Washington.

Here a very steep change of grade is handled with aplomb. The more geometrical treatment is kept from looking overly formal by the pleasingly naturalistic plantings that integrate the garden with the woodlands beyond. Although the repeated-theme plantings are formally spaced, the plants themselves are so well used that their own architectural strength is emphasized rather than dominated by the beautifully crafted hardscape. Israelit garden, designed by Michael Schultz, Portland, Oregon.

with the surrounding woodlands. Because the lot is small and the neighbors are near, the beds and borders are rather narrow. To compensate, we wasted no space on grass, but gave the entire lot over to the garden. The planting areas are divided by wide, graveled paths and seating areas, and every available inch has been planted. The result, thanks to the preponderance of woody plants, is extremely easy to care for. Thanks as well to an abundance of perennials, bulbs, and vines, the garden is already colorful and attractive in every season.

Gardens and Habitat

Gardens and Habitat

chapter 7

Until the past decade or so, the majority of garden designers largely ignored such factors as geography, climate, and existing native flora, imposing instead a standardized "ideal" template on any and every site.

There were of course outstanding exceptions, but all across the United States (and in many other countries), thousands of inappropriate gardens can be found to prove the point. Like the mythical retentive yet well drained soil so warmly recommended by traditional garden writers, a theoretically ideal garden situation is remarkably hard to duplicate in real life. It is particularly difficult when garden and natural habitat overlap. Traditionally, designers began by making major alterations to a given site, eliminating native plants, changing grades without regard to the original rise or fall of the setting, and usually attempting to change the basic soil type and texture as well. Although modern design trends do not preclude any of these activities, most current work reflects a deeper awareness of and appreciation for the natural conditions of each site.

Mountains, water, and forests dominate the Pacific Northwest and profoundly influence garden design. The lush abundance of the mountain meadows, where hundreds of plants are tightly sandwiched into interlayered, cooperative communities that share ground and resources, offers garden makers a practical and beautiful role model. Balsamroot (*Balsamorhiza* species) on Dog Mountain, Oregon.

Natural ponds and bogs are complex ecosystems that include the layered shrubs and perennials at the water's edge, as well as deep- and shallow-water inhabitants such as water lilies.

Instead of filling in or draining persistently damp areas, we create bog gardens. Where natural slopes are unworkable as garden beds, we edit native plantings that live happily there or make minor modifications of grade that allow us to develop planting spaces that do not create abrupt or obviously artificial transitions between the garden and the wild. Rather than eliminating native plants and beginning with the designers' "fresh slate," we incorporate the existing flora wherever possible, showcasing the handsomest in ways that emphasize their best qualities. Increasingly, too, if wild habitat adjoins our property, our planting patterns will reflect or echo that wild flora as well as our own taste. In fact, the majority of naturalistic borders refer directly to regional habitat, both visually and in terms of the chosen plant palette, and it is rare to find such a garden that does not combine natives with traditional border plants.

Until recently, those who wished to preserve existing habitat on their properties would hesitate to mix garden and wild plants. Proponents of wild gardening often argue that it is ecologically misguided to introduce exotic plants into a natural environment. Where large tracts of pristine habitat remain, this attitude is admirable indeed. However, most of us are gardening in degraded habitat at best, on land that has been logged or developed, possibly many times, before we came to it. Gardens in urban and suburban settings may adjoin a fractional piece of original habitat, which the designers might want to emphasize or emulate or incorporate into their gardens. In rural situations, new-growth woods are often full of invasive weeds from all over the world. Once the original ecological balance has been severely disturbed, any action we take that leads toward improving the site or setting as a naturalistic

Where intermittent streams leave garden soil soggy, artificial ponds can be created by amplifying that natural base. The large grasses planted at the bottom of this garden blend almost imperceptibly into beach grasses, making a seamless visual transition between the natural beach habitat and the lower garden. Garden designed by Eryl Morton, Victoria, British Columbia.

garden space may not be authentically restorative but can almost certainly be described as remedial.

The maritime gardens of Cascadia are in the vanguard of this movement, mingling habitat with artful, expressive gardens in an eco-sensitive manner, creating a new genre that serves plants (and often creatures) as well as people. A noteworthy garden where the overall design has been heavily influenced by such concerns can be found in Orting, Washington, sited on a high ridge overlooking the rolling farmlands of the Puyallup River valley, with territorial views of Mount Rainier to the east. In this favored spot, T. Emmott and Ione Chase have been gardening for close to fifty years. Now approaching their nineties, both were born and raised in this neck of the woods, and both are deeply committed to encouraging and preserving the native flora. Ione, whose eye and hand shaped much of the extensive garden, was raised a few miles away from this spot. Emmott grew up in Electron, Washington, and worked for Puget Power for many years. His job gave him access to hundreds of native plants, which he rescued from areas slated to be clear-cut for power-line paths.

Although the Chase garden site is quite large, only about 4 or 5 acres are under cultivation, since much of the land slopes too steeply to be worked. Instead the spreading acres below the house preserve their vistas and guarantee visual privacy. Logged back in 1908, mature second growth—firs, cedar and hemlock, bigleaf maple and cottonwood—now towers above an intricately interwoven understory of vine maples, huckleberries, and salal. Here and there bull timber appears; these trees were too small for removal at the turn of the century. In those days loggers left such trees in place, rather than waste their energy removing them (more of a consideration in the pre-chainsaw era), and as a result the Chases' woods have the feel of old-growth forest.

A graveled streambed meanders peacefully through an open section of the garden backed by forest. The sculptural Japanese maples are echoed by slender vine maples at the forest fringe. Chase garden, Orting, Washington.

A local designer, Rex Zumwalt, was asked in the early 1950s to create an open garden with a Japanese simplicity near the house. Here Japanese maples are set like sculpture amid great sweeps of ground cover plants, many of them natives. Ione Chase took Zumwalt's theme and carried it out in every direction. Now an open meadow studded with wildflowers emulates the alpine meadows of Mount Rainier. As the garden approaches the woods, plantings of rhododendrons and azaleas blend into huckleberry, native dogwoods, and ocean spray *(Holodiscus discolor)*.

The Chases' goal has long been to encourage wild-flowers as much as possible. Over the years they have filled the skirts of the woods with trilliums, collecting ripe seed every year and sowing it carefully. The same has been done with dogtooth violets *(Erythronium* species*)*, fairy bells *(Disporum smithii)*, false Solomon's seal *(Smilacina racemosa)*, foam flower *(Tiarella trifoliata)*, star flower *(Trientalis latifolia)*, and violets *(Viola glabella* and ever-green *V. sempervirens)*. Wild ginger *(Asarum marmoratum)* multiplies in several areas, while stands of pallid coral root *(Corallorhiza maculata)* open ghostly orchid sprays. Earliest to bloom, kittentails *(Synthyris reniformis)* produce pale blue sprays of white-eyed flowers at winter's end in the natural moss garden, where carpets of vanilla leaf *(Achlys triphylla)* are interrupted by a wide variety of native ferns and spiky, vicious-looking devil's-club *(Oplopanax horridus)*. Everywhere, nurse logs left from original logging have supported new trees that are now coming of age. The Chases observe that when they began the garden, nearly fifty years ago, the nurse logs were twice as high as they are now, when their substance has been depleted by the growing saplings.

Junipers and heathers interlace naturalistically near the house, where territorial views extend the garden to the horizon. Loosely woven tiers of shrubs and trees call the eye upward, linking the garden back to the forest beyond. Chase garden, Orting, Washington.

Meadows and Lawns

Where gardens spill into natural meadows, the main job is keeping the native plants free of invaders. This is trickiest in suburban areas where yard weeds and exotics, including many European wildflowers, seed themselves everywhere. Even in rural areas, most terrain has been disturbed at least once over the past century. Clear-cutting and development have left many a scar on the wild, and more often, we are dealing with a mixed legacy rather than unspoiled habitat. In those rare cases where we do have the opportunity to garden near pristine meadows, it is important to be very selective about what plants we bring in. Seeing the way that purple loosestrife has filled marshes and bogs from Maine to Minnesota has taught a lot of gardeners that we need to be knowledgeable about unleashing aggressive plants where they may escape to the wild.

In the Pacific Northwest, the noxious weed list includes English ivy *(Hedera helix)*, a rampant spreader that is also bird-sown. This pest plant has been spotted deep in national forest preserves, and is omnipresent in suburban and rural settings. Another all-too-willing worker on the hit list is herb Robert *(Geranium robertianum)*. A garden herb once used medicinally, this rapid seeder makes lacy circles of airy, delicate-looking foliage, but manages to utterly block all challengers. This smothering ability is a good habit in a ground cover, but when the ground cover gets away and starts infiltrating the woods, we have a problem. Herb Robert spreads in all the usual ways, but the most serious vector is human: Hundreds of hikers carry seed from gardens or roadsides into the forests and national parks. The tiny seed rides in on shoe seams, in the mud caked into hiking-boot soles, and

Where the garden borders the woods, ground covers of native plants create wide sweeps of ever-changing color beneath the rugged trunks of maturing trees. Here native red currant *(Ribes sanguineum)* and dogwood *(Cornus nuttallii)* are underplanted with trilliums, star flowers, and dogtooth violets *(Erythronium* species)*. Chase garden, Orting, Washington.

even in the hems of trousers, sprouting happily wherever it falls. The ubiquity of Scotch broom and Himalayan giant blackberry (imported by Luther Burbank himself) makes the lesson clear. If there are any doubts whatsoever about a given plant's suitability for a site that needs protection, a call to your county agricultural extension agent will clear them up immediately.

In suburban and rural settings where natural meadow has been replaced by lawns, there are some good reasons for replicating meadows of one kind or another. For one, faced with feeding, weeding, and mowing large expanses of grass, many naturalistic gardeners prefer to replace the endless turf with less demanding plants. However, doing this successfully requires some forethought and knowledge if we are not to face the bitter disappointment of a weedy mess and more work than the lawn demanded. Meadow mixtures are often sold (in cute little cans) that promise instant luxuriance, but most are all but guaranteed to fail. Blended from a handful of persistent wildflowers, most also contain aggressive grasses that will soon take over, choking out the flowers. The few perennials included are rarely strong enough to established themselves before the sweep of grasses smothers them. Most gardeners end up mowing their meadows in despair, overwhelmed by the race between weeds and unwanted grasses.

If you do want to make a garden meadow, mountain meadows are a good model to study, for they hold a large assortment of plants, most of them tough perennials that can hold their own against encroaching grasses. The

Mountain meadows demonstrate a richness of interlayered planting that can be adapted for garden meadows.

grasses in mountain meadows tend to be clumpers, which share space more willingly than crabgrass or other running species. The meadow model might also encourage us to play around with some of the handsome ornamental grasses, like clumping fescues and low-growing, seed-spangled poas, which don't get tall enough to choke out neighbors. It is also perfectly appropriate to weave in bigger grasses like silky *Stipa tenuissima*, which produces quantities of seed for the birds as well as plants for the gardener eager for more.

If you like the wilder meadow look, consider using some tall maiden grasses *(Miscanthus* species*)* as well as dwarf or full-sized pampas grasses like airy *Cortaderia richardii* (called plumed tussocks grass for obvious reasons). Before planting a lot of big grasses, however, it is worth calling your local extension service again to ask whether any of the grasses you are considering might be a problem. In some areas (notably Northern California), some of the pampas grasses have naturalized so successfully that they are endangering native grasses. In the cooler Northwest this is not a problem, since so many of the larger grasses bloom too late to set viable seed. Still, the point is well worth checking if you aren't sure about seed timing or viability in your region.

To succeed in replacing grasses with meadow flowers, we need to get rid of all the turf. This can be done by stripping sod (removing it in strips, which can be composted), or by tilling it under. Once the grass is gone,

Anemones, false hellebore *(Veratrum viride)*, lupines, monkey flowers, and a dozen other species mingle in the living meadow tapestry.

Trimming this small meadow is simplified by an edging of the naturalized native wildflower, *Limnanthes douglasii*, a happy performer that does not resent the incursions of a sit-down mower. Garden of Phoebe Noble, Sidney, British Columbia.

replacement with a blend of annuals and perennials can begin. It is almost impossible to replace a lost meadow with its original inhabitants, especially after the soil has been disturbed and/or replaced. In suburban situations, where wind-blown weeds will make any attempt to naturalize futile, it is not even worth trying. There some of the best perennials for meadow mixtures are the yarrows *(Achillea* species), which come in a large range of colors. In sunny, well-drained sites, creeping thymes and chamomile, oregano and prostrate mints can all be used. Meadow or ox-eye daisies *(Chrysanthemum leucanthemum)* are stubborn place-holders, as are blue chicory *(Cichorium intybus)* and Queen Anne's lace *(Daucus carota).* Native annual wildflowers such as sunny golden

California poppies *(Eschscholzia californica)*, fried egg flower *(Limnanthes douglasii)*, and baby blue eyes *(Nemophila menziesii)* generally replace themselves well. As a final work-saver, edge the meadow with plants that take regular mowing in stride, like many of the wild and ornamental grasses, or wildflowers like fried egg flower.

Gardening on the Beach

Cascadia's long, wandering coastline offers thousands of gardeners a chance to integrate their imported plantings with natives. The outer coast, with its big surf and sandy beaches, represents a fairly fragile environment that supports a limited number of species, and in most cases the native flora is best left as undisturbed as possible. In gardens farther inland, where bays and sounds and inlets create more sheltered shoreline, far more complex garden plantings can reasonably be attempted. Again, where native plantings are intact, they are best left that way to prevent erosion and create a protective wind belt for the garden. Where plants have been replaced with bulkheads, jetties, and walls, anything goes. However, we can usefully look at what grows naturally in such settings, taking our cues from nature. Wild grasses give way quickly to mixed thickets of wild roses, and salal competes with willows, alders, and twiggy dogwoods.

On Vancouver Island in British Columbia, designer Cyril Hume gardens on Roberts Point, where the last local traces of old-growth woods remain. He lives in a historic neighborhood, on land homesteaded by his grandparents at the turn of the century. The cottage they built sits just a few feet above the windy beach, and plants that can't tolerate salt spray are short-lived here. A windbreak hedge runs between beach and garden, woven from intertwined native shrubs. Snowberry bush *(Symphoricarpos* species*)*, foamy ocean spray *(Holodiscus discolor)*, and wiry Nootka rose *(Rosa nutkana)* are tightly interwoven, along with a native crab apple kept as a shrub by hard pruning. Nearer to the house, bridal veil *(Spiraea vanhouttei)* joins the mix, making an all-but-impenetrable barrier that protects the garden plantings. A winding path leads up from the beach, breaching the hedge to enter a small meadow that spreads out before a fringe of arbutus trees *(Arbutus menziesii;* they're called madronas, stateside).

The little meadow has always been kept intact, first by Cyril's grandmother, who encouraged the proliferation of the native fawn lily *(Erythronium* species*)* and chocolate lily *(Fritillaria lanceolata)*. Now great sheets of fawn lily spangle the short grass, preceded by masses of crocus and hardy cyclamen added by Cyril. "My grandmother pointed out a single clump of chocolate lily, which has now multiplied extensively," notes Cyril, who claims the reason it performs so well is because he leaves it alone. "I do seed the erythroniums about, but the chocolate lily is best untouched," he explains. He recently learned that the meadow is a very old midden, left by native people long ago. "The archaeologist told me it is classified as a site of archaeological interest, and best left undisturbed, so it's just as well that we have always liked it best that

Coastal environments are fragile, and native plantings are best left undisturbed. If need be, native grasses and shrubs may be supplemented with others of their own kind to create windbreaks and shelter belts for gardens.

Native snowberry *(Symphoricarpos species)*, foamy ocean spray *(Holodiscus discolor)*, and wiry Nootka rose *(Rosa nutkana)* weave together into a tightly weather-proof barrier for the small meadow and garden tucked just a few feet above the beach. Every five years, the hedge is cut back hard to keep it dense and twiggy and to preserve the ocean views from the house. Garden of Cyril Hume, Sidney, British Columbia.

way," he says with a smile, adding, "Apparently, my crocus and cyclamen are OK, however."

In leaving the little meadow natural, he recognizes that his grandmother continued what was probably a tradition of centuries' standing. "The site quite obviously had meaning to people long before my grandparents were here." Cyril, whose specialty is in recreating historically accurate gardens, is quick to appreciate such points. Indeed, he is presently engaged in a movement to protect

Left natural since the accompanying cottage was built early in the century, this small meadow was once a meeting place for native people, who gathered here many centuries ago. In spring the short grass is starred with thousands of native fawn lilies (*Erythronium* species) and chocolate lilies (*Fritillaria lanceolata*), which do not at all mind the company of imported crocus and cyclamen. The garden's carefully sculpted beds echo the lines and forms of the clustered islands that lie just offshore. Garden of Cyril Hume, Sidney, British Columbia.

his historical neighborhood and its trees. Developers want to make huge suburbs on Roberts Point, replacing its old homes, as well as stands of trees, which include the final one percent of the native Douglas fir population in the city of Sidney. Such battles are sadly common these days, led as often as not by gardeners who respect the native flora as much as they enjoy their garden exotics.

Tropicalismo
for Temperate Gardens

Tropicalismo
for Temperate Gardens

chapter 8

Of all the currently emergent naturalistic design schools, the most dazzlingly different is a showboat called *tropicalismo*. Indeed, many would argue fiercely that tropicalismo has no business being included under the

same heading. However, although their connections are not immediately obvious to everyone, it can be demonstrated that tropicalismo and several other hardy-tropicals-based design schools reflect precisely the same planting

principles as naturalistic garden making. Plant-centered and determinedly overstated, tropicalismo is based on drama and high contrast. Hardy tropicals, exotic foliage plants that tolerate temperate climates, are the heavy hitters here, though in most tropicalismo gardens they mingle with flamboyant plants from every corner of the world. In the Pacific Northwest, where many native woodland plants have decidedly tropical-looking leaves, devotees of this young genre have enthusiastically embraced both the imports and the local flora.

Tropical plants have long been incorporated into ornamental borders, even in climates where they needed

---

Oversized plants, arranged to offer powerful contrasts of form and texture, create the naturalistic look called tropicalismo. *This salsa-based school of garden design celebrates the flamboyant, making garden visits both joyful and transformational. Garden of Linda Cochran, Bainbridge Island, Washington.*

cold storage over the winter to survive. One significant difference between traditional and contemporary foliage gardens is that the newest of them are based on genuinely hardy plants. Finding these has taken some of tropicalismo's greatest advocates to the high mountains of Chile, New Zealand, and South Africa in search of fresh possibilities. In the Pacific Northwest and increasingly in other warm-winter regions of the country—especially in

Where dry summers are the norm, naturalistic gardens may be open and spare rather than lush and green. Plants from places that share the modified Mediterranean climate (such as South Africa, New Zealand, Chile, and the coastal Pacific Northwest) look convincingly at home when arranged together. Garden of Harlan Hand, El Cerrito, California.

USDA hardiness Zones 8 to 10 where a generous number of them are reasonably hardy—hardy tropicals and exotic lookalikes are the hottest trend in haute garden design.

On both East and West Coasts, colorist borders based on tropical foliage mingle lanky gingers with variegated corn, their tall stalks amazingly similar in construction, but ending in the ginger's case in a fizz of fragrant, orchid-like flowers. Taros of all kinds are appearing in sunny gardens, both tender black ones and hardier green ones that survive Zone 8 winters with aplomb. Angelwinged Rex begonias and fantastically patterned elephant ears (*Caladium* species) enliven staid mixtures of hostas and ferns in shaded borders. Colocasias and alocasias, aloes, and all manner of hot country plants are being woven into bedding schemes with the same fervid enthusiasm once displayed by Victorian gardeners.

The multitude of ways in which designers use these plants is as fascinating as the plants themselves. On the West Coast, where foliage plants tend to thrive, several related design schools are developing simultaneously with tropicalismo. Built like tropicalismo upon bold, large-scale plants with dramatic foliage, hardy-tropicals gardens similarly evoke the jungle understory, but with more restraint, expressing an architectural appreciation for line and mass. Many hardy-tropicals gardens are cool green sanctuaries, wondrous webs woven with potent forms and a wide range of textures.

Mediterranean models are equally popular, especially in drier, sunnier coastal gardens. Some echo the maquis, with lovely masses of low shrubs like rosemary, lavender, sage, and cistus, punctuated by taller junipers and billowy brooms. Many of these fit comfortably under the naturalistic umbrella, incorporating the same trademark layering

Northwestern tropicalismo gardens often draw upon less commonly tapped traditions such as Thai gardens, or those of Mexico and Brazil. This shot, taken from a Balinese tea hut, overlooks a shapely silk floss tree *(Albizia julibrissin)*, which interlayers dramatically with Pacific Island reed grass *(Miscanthus floridulus)*, Mexican mock orange *(Choisya ternata)*, and a purple Venetian sumac *(Cotinus coggygria* 'Velvet Cloak'). Garden of Ron Wagoner & Nani Wadoops, Portland, Oregon.

and emphasizing the sculptural qualities of the plants. Natives like rabbit brush *(Chrysothamnus viscidiflorus)*, creosote bush *(Larrea tridentata)*, and numerous desert sages blend into such schemes with ease, combining readily with traditional Mediterranean garden plants such as rosemary and lavender.

Still other hardy-tropical designers prefer European models that rely on hardscape and architecture. In their gardens, classic columns and graveled sweeps austerely decorated with a few sculpturally placed palms contrast

suddenly with romantic tangles of jasmine and roses tumbling over an enclosing wall. The plant palette tends to be very limited in these gardens, where form and color take precedence.

Though similarly celebrating dramatic form and exotic foliage, the tropicalismo garden glories even more in gigantism and extravagance. It differs as well in an emphasis on true panic, that neck-prickling recognition of nature's dominance. Tropicalismo gardeners delight in vegetative enclosure that overwhelms, creating gardens where plants are not restricted to beds and borders. In California, the Berkeley-based sculptor Marcia Donahue likens this style (of which her own garden is a choice example) to the new zoos, where animals roam free and people are confined to paths.

Perhaps the key element that sets these gardens apart from those of the more traditional foliage-based design schools is their source. All of these developing schools have roots in South American countries, where gardening with tropicals means using native plants. As the concepts and plants moved northward, stopovers in San Francisco and Seattle added a distinctly North American twist. Like Brazilian musical tropicalismo, the movement that begat world music, garden tropicalismo is about fusion and

Native scouler willows (Salix scouleriana) anchor these luxuriant tropicalismo borders firmly to their setting, tying the garden to the surrounding skyline. Mixtures of native shrubs and trees are preserved in many areas throughout the garden, making visual links to the greenbelt between neighboring houses. Garden of Linda Cochran, Bainbridge Island, Washington.

going beyond old patterns. Tropicalismo thus incorporates plants from everywhere and anywhere, so long as they enjoy each other's company and provide the visual effect the gardener wants. Hardy-tropicals gardens are based on plant form and foliage patterns rather than on flowers. Though flowers do play their part (and often a significant one), it is the flow and interplay of shape and texture that inform the design and create ongoing visual interest.

Adventurous Northwestern gardeners are currently experimenting with all sorts of tropicals, not just those from South America. African banana trees mingle with spiky New Zealand flax. Chinese windmill palms merge with Tasmanian tree ferns and European giant reed grasses. As a result, plants with fascinating foliage are all the rage. Once condemned by association with Victorian bedding-out schemes as coarse and rather obvious, variegated cannas are now urgently in demand. Palm trees, a former gardening solecism, are snatched out of nurseries as fast as they appear. Just a few years ago, understated plants and white gardens were the hallmarks of good taste. Today, the bigger and bolder the better. Up and down both coasts, quiet plants in cool pastels are being ousted by brazen bruisers in blazing colors. Although few people are ripping out their old gardens and starting entirely anew, many of us are revising our accustomed plant palettes to include hardy tropicals. However, unless we can do this with exceptional finesse, the values of the old styles may be seriously compromised. In itself this cultural clash is not a bad thing, since it forces us to think afresh about what we want for and from our gardens.

The first push of any new movement usually involves a certain amount of overstatement, simply to make a point. Part of the point here is to break away from old visual templates that have shaped our internalized, often subconscious, concept of what a garden could and should be. English borders and European formalism are perhaps the strongest of these, with Asian Zen gardens making a powerful third. In some regions, notably the Pacific Northwest, regional pride in an extraordinary native flora has further complicated all these influences, resulting in several unique design schools. Curiously enough, it is the Northwestern naturalistic gardens that lend themselves most readily to the influx of tropicalismo.

Based heavily on native plants and natural plant relationships, Northwestern naturalistic gardens employ a multilayered planting style that convincingly evokes the wild. Many are dominated by dramatic natives like madronas *(Arbutus menziesii)* and garry oaks *(Quercus garryana)*, sculptural trees that mimic exotic, hot-country plants. Add large-leaved perennials like the cut-leaf coltsfoot *(Petasites frigidus* var. *palmatum)*; tall, pleated false hellebore *(Veratrum viride)*; giant cow parsnip *(Heracleum lanatum)*; and umbrella plant *(Darmera peltata)*, and you have a framework that will quite easily support the introduction of a gunnera and a few bananas. Even those primitive looking Tasmanian tree ferns appear surprisingly at home, because the Northwestern coastal woods are full of rotting stumps, first topped by long-ago loggers and now topped again with lusty sword ferns. In silhouette it can be hard to tell which plant belongs and which came from halfway around the world. Northwestern followers of tropicalismo gardening have been known to assert that the flora that encompasses devil's-club *(Oplopanax horridus)*, a native woodlander that looks like it came from Mars, can take anything in stride.

Doubters often suggest that tropicalismo in particular is antithetical to regionalism. Philosophically, many gardeners believe that we should "garden where we live," employing regional architectural idioms, building materials, and plants to tie our gardens firmly to our specific settings. I myself have written about these ideas many times, and feel that they are indeed vital to creating gardens with a true sense of place. However, several arguments may expand our thinking along these lines. First, gardens in urban (and even suburban) settings may have no natural context whatsoever. When your garden tree line is replaced by city skyline, anything goes. Both naturalistic and tropicalismo gardens do, in fact, work wonderfully in totally artificial environments, instantly transporting us from the urban to the wild. What's more, regionalism can be interpreted narrowly or broadly. Most often we think in terms of what is or has been true about a given place. However, a more expansive concept of regionalistic gardening could include the possibilities presented by that region. In the Pacific Northwest, for example, plants from all over the temperate world can be grown without resorting to complex winter protection strategies. Where hardy tropicals really are hardy, why not incorporate them into our gardens, if we can do so convincingly?

This brings up a further point that proponents of tropicalismo find puzzling: Who is it exactly that we need to convince? Linda Cochran, whose large tropicalismo garden near Seattle has become an epicenter of the movement, questions the hidden assumptions about what makes a garden tasteful or tacky. "Everything depends on what kinds of art we find appealing," she asserts. "I enjoy Mexican and Southwestern art based on brilliant colors and strong contrasts, and my garden reflects that bias. I often

Dark-leaved 'Fascination' dahlias mingle with murky-red banana foliage, backed by rounded, deep-lobed rice paper plant, *Tetrapanax papyriferus*, and the steel blue, saw-toothed foliage of South African honey bush, *Melianthus major*. To eyes trained on tasteful English pastels, brazen combinations of colors and plants that reflect South American design influences can seem to threaten the canons of Good Taste. Garden of Linda Cochran, Bainbridge Island, Washington.

wonder what people mean when they say that this kind of garden doesn't look "right" with the native landscape, which in my case was logged-over brush. What was here originally was modified rain forest, so what I'm doing is actually closer to that model, in its lushness, than the Himalayan blackberries and Scotch broom that had taken over."

Cochran is also baffled by criticisms about the use of frankly tender plants that need to overwinter indoors. "Some plant Nazis get upset when we grow brugmansias and bananas, because these plants 'shouldn't' be hardy

here, yet nobody thinks it's wrong to dig and store dahlia tubers, here or anywhere else in the country. Why is it suspect when it's a banana?"

What's more, part of the tropicalismo mission is seeking out genuinely hardy forms of traditionally tender plants. In Cochran's Zone 8 garden, several bananas (forms of *Musa basjoo*) have survived several difficult winters in the garden. Hardy taros (*Colocasia* species) have come through nicely, though late to rise, and the longest-established Tasmanian tree fern didn't even drop its fronds despite a 3-foot fall of snow. Most of her considerable canna collection has proven root-hardy, and she is constantly experimenting with other marginal tropicals to find the toughest and most adaptable kinds.

Cochran finds it ironic that, by some osmotic process, anything considered an English border plant becomes perfectly acceptable to grow, whether its provenance is actually China, Australia, or the Arctic Circle. Many common border plants come from wildly exotic places, yet they don't create the controversy sparked by tree ferns or taro. "I think some people have trouble with the unfamiliar," she suggests. "Ideas from England and Europe are fine, but ideas from places like Mexico and Brazil, which have been overlooked in most horticultural circles, can seem threatening."

Exploring new ways of partnering plants can make for intense visual excitement. Sandwiched between two fuzzy-leaved *Rhododendron bureavii*, a broad-bladed and vividly striped New Zealand flax counterbalances the soft cascade of Chinese water grass, *Hakonechloa macra* 'Aureola'. Garden of Linda Cochran, Bainbridge Island, Washington.

Moreover, Cochran questions the critic's idea that a garden should look "right" for its setting. "If the purpose of your garden is simply decorative, to make your house look more like the rest of the neighborhood, maybe the point about trying to suit your context is legitimate," she concedes. "It also makes total sense if you are creating a habitat garden, or gardening in some perfect natural setting. But anywhere else, the choice is really yours. If your goal is to make magic, to create a different reality, then you employ whatever you need to get the effect you want."

In Portland, Oregon, plantsmen Sean Hogan and Parker Sanderson are filling their whole neighborhood with hardy tropicals. Not content to pack their own yard with wandering mutisias, hardy palms, and spiky agaves, they have spilled their garden out to the street, where it splashes merrily into parking strips and nearby lots. Hogan, who until recently worked as a horticulturalist at U.C. Berkeley's Botanical Garden, has a deep and abiding affection for the native flora of both California and the Northwest, but is equally fond of plants from all over the world. Among tropicalismo gardeners, Hogan is famous for his theories on zonal denial. "The idea is to plant everything you want to, and get people excited about the possibilities," he explains. "If plants die, you just replace them immediately. When people ask whether they made it, you lie."

He acknowledges that it makes for some touchy moments if you don't match replacements with care, and must try to convince a friend that those once-yellow flowers must have turned blue from cold. "In all seriousness," he continues, "this isn't about running down to the nearest houseplant store and loading up on goodies. A great deal of research is involved in traveling all over the world to find truly hardy tropicals. It means actively exploring in places like Chile and Brazil to find the southernmost habitat for desirable species, then selecting seed from the most adaptable forms we can find in nature. Lots of potential garden plants are out there. It's a matter of finding them and making them available for testing in garden settings."

A few years back, Hogan spent part of May at English garden writer Christopher Lloyd's garden, Great Dixter. "It was great fun to help unpack the tropicals, but it struck me that a lot of installation was involved, as it is in the hardy-tropicals gardens back east," he comments. Sophisticated English gardeners like Lloyd have been creating striking foliage effects with tropicals for years, as witness Lloyd's own book, *Foliage Plants*, published in 1973. "It's taken for granted in England that these terrific tropical foliage plants aren't hardy. People are quite willing to store them with care, or simply replace them each year."

Here in the Northwest, we are looking for something a bit different, Hogan feels. He echoes the sentiments of many when he says, "I'm not entirely comfortable with planting so much of the garden out in May and pulling it all out again for storage in October. I want more time." It isn't the extra work he grudges, however. "Many people will put dormant spray on a peach tree, which I won't do, but I'm willing to throw a blanket over my phormiums when frost is predicted," he acknowledges. "Still, I don't want a garden full of boxed plants in winter."

For Hogan, as for Cochran, part of the point of hardy tropicals is the magic they create. "When we make garden rooms, why not furnish them with wit and imagination? Isn't it fun to turn a corner and be transported to a world of your choice?"

Hogan also agrees that hardy-tropical gardens work brilliantly in small spaces. "In Portland, most of us have very small gardens, often surrounded by urban structures. When your plot is only 20 feet square, our natural inclination is to use small-scale design, but think about what happens when you line a small room with small furniture. If instead you use a few oversized pieces, perhaps a huge couch and a giant chair, the furnishings create their own ambience. Using just a few outsized, boldly textured plants gives a neutral small space an immediate sense of intimacy."

Northwestern hardy-tropical gardeners tend to use their emphatic plants more adventurously and more playfully than do the English, though that is changing. "In 1989, when I gave Christopher Lloyd a tour of some Bay Area tropical gardens, he went nuts," chuckles Hogan. "Right after that, he went home and ripped out his rose garden and replaced it with hardy tropicals. Maybe we reinspired him."

The insouciance of many Bay Area tropicals gardens is indeed inspiring, and their effects are emulated beyond the range of the plants they often employ. In Berkeley, Marcia Donahue has made a potently influential garden

Tropicalismo gardens gain an exuberant, playful quality when designers emphasize the improbable, astonishing, and even magical aspects of plant communities. Using enormous foliage plants like gunneras, cannas, giant joe-pye weeds, and tall grasses creates an Alice-in-Wonderland experience for visitors. Garden of Linda Cochran, with column sculpture by Little and Lewis, Bainbridge Island, Washington.

that successfully combines garden art—whether her own stone pieces, or her partner Mark Bulwinkle's fraught metalwork—with artfully placed tropicals. Donahue is always pushing the envelope, growing plants on the edge of hardiness and placing them to perfection. Just now she is experimenting with tropical begonias, many of which are lusty, prodigious plants with smoky foliage and vivid flowers. Another current favorite is a massive Ecuadorean eggplant relative, *Solanum quitoense*, whose thick, velvety purple leaves are veined "like the map of a tropical river system, in khaki, purple, and dark green" and so prominent, the effect is "almost frighteningly powerful." Her garden has been well stocked with outsized plants for years, because she enjoys the way "gigantism allows us to be *inside* the garden."

Donahue finds gargantuan plants "delightfully preposterous," because "the tiny-Alice effect is really appealing to the child in us." She adds, "Pleasing yourself is what you get to do in your own garden. It's one of the few places where you have any control." Making gardens that threaten our sense of control (yet are well grown) works for Donahue: "It has to do with the force of nature that is you; people do forget that they are creating works of art. You are part of your own genius loci."

Exotic, exuberant garden styles are not to every taste, nor do they suit every setting or style of architecture. However, their large scale and generous scope make them tremendous fun to create, no matter where you garden. Even if you don't elect to replace your roses with red bananas and palm trees, a few emphatic foliage plants (like aralias, sumacs, elders, and catalpas) can restimulate tame or tired gardens. Altering the overall balance between hardscape—the man-made elements such as patios, terraces, arbors, and pergolas—and plants will similarly revitalize formal gardens that have achieved a stultifying stasis. In tropicalismo gardens, plants are in the ascendant, whereas English and European traditions require that the hand of man predominate. If you choose not to alter a leaf of your own garden, you may nonetheless be refreshed in spirit through immersion in a tropicalismo garden, where old ideas about who is in charge and why are turned upside down. Like Alice returning from Looking-glass Land, we see the garden anew, a mind-altering experience that can only benefit our gardens and our ability to rejoice in plants.

Plant-driven design alters the internal balance of a garden, shifting the attention away from hardscape and the formality of straight lines. It is still possible to create very orderly effects, and even to set them off with insouciance. Here a large bed (nicknamed "the savannah") of *Stipa tenuissima* adds a strong flavor of the wild to the scene, which grows progressively less structured as it melts into native woods in the background. Garden of Linda Cochran, Bainbridge Island, Washington.

PLANT PORTRAIT

Naturally, not every garden is suited to an infusion of tropical foliage plants. However, many established borders are based on plants that lend themselves readily to expansion in this direction. Any plant with outsized foliage can be reconsidered in this light, from rhododendrons to rhubarbs. *Fatsia japonica* and gold-spotted aucubas take on an entirely new look when paired with other big-leaved beauties. Raid the kitchen garden for towering angelicas, giant rhubarbs, and feathery fennel. Pacific gunneras share border space readily with Northwestern skunk cabbages.

Tree Ferns, *Dicksonia* species

The Tasmanian tree fern (*Dicksonia antarctica*, Zone 8) is the hardiest of the dicksonias. This ancient plant is found throughout the forests of southeastern Australia, though plants hailing from the island of Tasmania (where snow is not uncommon) seem to be the toughest when transplanted here. These giant terrestrial ferns mostly arrive in this country as escapees from the massive deforestation that is fast reducing native Australian woodlands. Although they are quite slow-growing, Tasmanian tree ferns have an amazing ability to re-root. Regional nursery folks are learning that even clear-cut stumps can be rooted well enough to plant out in a single season. Since spore-grown plants take years to achieve a stately size, a ready market for the leftovers of Australian logging is developing in Canada and the United States.

In garden terms, young tree ferns are quick to establish in any decent garden soil, and mature plants transplant with ease. In cool, Northwestern gardens, dicksonias tolerate the local equivalent of full sun, but where summers are warmer, tree ferns appreciate the same shady conditions that please lesser ferns. Their nutritional wants are modest, and plenty of compost, good drainage, and adequate water are all that is needed to keep them happy for decades.

Tasmanian tree ferns are understory plants that adapt well to what passes for sun in the cool, coastal Northwest. Elsewhere partial shade is recommended, lest those complex foliage fronds crisp up during summer heat waves. They look exotic in a garden setting, but in the woods they bear an amazing resemblance to a sword fern growing out of a logged-off stump. Garden of Linda Cochran, Bainbridge Island, Washington.

PLANT PORTRAIT

Sumac, *Rhus glabra*

Wild sumacs have oversized, long-fingered foliage that looks excitingly tropical, even though they are native throughout much of North America. Most species have velvety stems that look like antlers in winter, and nearly all offer persistent and sizzling autumn foliage coloring. Some are too rowdy for border duty, but a few are mannerly enough to earn a lasting and valued place in a hardy-tropicals garden. The northern smooth sumac, *Rhus glabra*, offers terrific fall color and glossy, wine-red winter stems, as well as a summerful of shaggy green leaves. In gardens this enthusiastic shrub can reach 12 or even 20 feet, but is often held under 10 feet by competition and overall conditions. To keep it small you can also cut it back hard every few years. Over time this weakens any plant, but then, some plants can use a little weakening. Cut-back plants will be more compact, and the individual leaflets can exceed 3 feet in length.

Fragrant lemon sumac, *Rhus aromatica*, is another excellent choice, especially for those with smaller gardens. This East Coast native grows 2 to 3 feet tall and spreads slowly into large colonies over time, unless its young sprouts are removed. This one also has outstanding fall color, especially in its cutleaf form, 'Laciniata'. Pale yellow, lemon-scented flowers appear in summer, followed by reddish berries.

Unexpected juxtapositions make for high visual drama in tropicalismo gardens, where naturalistic relationships are treated with an intriguing blend of respect and playful experimentation. This rapidly expanding school of design is stretching our assumptions, forcing us to rethink what we want for and from our gardens. They also remind us that the future is wide open. Garden of Roger Raiche, Berkeley, California.

First and foremost, I thank Ann Lovejoy for inviting me into the garden fast lane. Her infectious enthusiasm, ever-present positive energy, and quick e-mail response time make her a terrific partner to work with. She's pointed me to some of the finest gardens on this planet. I am deeply grateful to all the gardeners in the United States and Canada who have dedicated so much of their life's energy to creating beautiful naturalistic gardens and who have allowed me to photograph them. These are truly generous people, and it shows in their gardens. I would also like to thank the following: Katsuhiko Mizuno, for his inspirational guidance; Molly Sullivan, for her intrepid assistance finding images off the beaten path; Betsy Amster, my agent, for her invaluable skills and advice; Gary Luke, our editor at Sasquatch Books, for believing in this project; my parents, for their love; and my wife Donatella, for her support during the many months of shooting and editing.

—ALLAN MANDELL

Printed in Hong Kong.
Distributed in Canada by Raincoast Books Ltd.
02 01 00 99   5 4 3 2

Cover and interior design: Karen Schober
Leaf illustration: Lily Lee

Cover photograph: Madrona garden, designed by Michael Schultz and Geoff Beasley, Sherwood, Oregon
Title page photograph: Garden of Robin Hopper and Judi Dyelle, Metchosin, British Columbia
Pages 30-31: Garden of Ernie and Marietta O'Byrne, Eugene, Oregon
Pages 46-47: Sunrise Gardens, designed by Bobbie Garthwaite and Joe Sullivan, Bainbridge Island, Washington
Pages 66-67: Portland Japanese Garden, Portland, Oregon
Pages 84-85: Garden of Carmen Varcoe, Victoria, British Columbia
Pages 102-103: Garden of Lucy and Fred Hardiman, Portland, Oregon
Pages 122-123: Garden of Carmen Varcoe, Victoria, British Columbia
Pages 137-138: Garden of Roger Raiche, Berkeley, California
Photograph of Ann Lovejoy: Joel Sackett
Photograph of Allan Mandell: Donatella Rossi

Library of Congress Cataloging in Publication Data
Lovejoy, Ann, 1951–
Naturalistic gardening : reflecting the planting patterns of nature / Ann Lovejoy : photographs by Allan Mandell.
p. cm.
Includes index.
ISBN 1-57061-120-3
1. Natural gardens, American. 2. Natural landscaping. I. Title.
SB457.53.L68   1998
712.6—dc21   98-6130
Sasquatch Books
615 Second Avenue • Seattle, Washington 98104
(206) 467-4300
books@SasquatchBooks.com • http://www.SasquatchBooks.com

Sasquatch Books publishes high-quality adult nonfiction and children's books related to the Northwest (Alaska to San Francisco). For more information about our titles, contact us at the address above, or view our site on the World Wide Web.